AUTOBIOGRAPHY

NAN A. TALESE

DOUBLEDAY

New York   London   Toronto

Sydney   Auckland

HELMUT NEWTON

AUTOBIOGRAPHY

PUBLISHED BY NAN A. TALESE
AN IMPRINT OF DOUBLEDAY
a division of Random House, Inc.
1745 Broadway, New York, NY 10019

DOUBLEDAY is a registered trademark of Random House, Inc.

Autobiography was first published in 2002 under the title *Autobiographie*
by C. Bertelsmann Verlag, Munich.
All photographs are the property of Helmut Newton.

While all of the incidents in this book are true, some of the names of the individuals
have been changed in order to protect their privacy.

Book design by Marysarah Quinn

Library of Congress Cataloging-in-Publication Data
Newton, Helmut, 1920–
Autobiography / Helmut Newton.— 1st ed.
p. cm.
1. Newton, Helmut, 1920– 2. Photographers— Biography.
3. Fashion photography. I. Title.

TR140.N313.A3 2003
770'.92—dc21
[B]   2003040255

ISBN 0-385-50807-7

Copyright © 2002 by Helmut Newton

All Rights Reserved
PRINTED IN THE UNITED STATES OF AMERICA
November 2003

FIRST EDITION
1   3   5   7   9   10   8   6   4   2

For Max, Claire, and June

CONTENTS

Prologue   *1*

PART I: THE BIOGRAPHY

PART II: THE PHOTOGRAPHS

PROLOGUE

I WAS THREE or four years old, lying in my bed in my parents' apartment on the Innsbruckerstrasse. It was night, it was always night—a lot of my memories are of night. My nurse, my Kinderfräulein, is getting ready to go out, and she is half naked. She has on a slip, and she is sitting in front of the mirror. There was a light above the mirror in my room. She is putting on makeup, and she looks very pretty. I know that this was the first time that I had seen, that I remember seeing, a half-naked young woman in front of a mirror.

My parents went out a lot at night to parties and nightclubs, and my mother always came in before I went to sleep to say good night. I can remember feeling her bare arms—because sometimes she was wearing a cocktail or evening dress—and I used to get very excited and stimulated. But, then, I thought my mother was a wonderful-looking woman and the most desirable person there was.

There was a little lamp with a very soft light beside my bed. Sometimes my mother came in before she had put her dress on; she wore pearls and a slip and a bra underneath. The slip was satin, flesh-colored. It was always flesh-colored, never black. She would come in and sit down by my bedside.

She smelled good; she always wore Chanel No. 5. I can remember putting my arms around her and feeling her skin.

She was quite buxom. She had big breasts and round arms and round shoulders, and she wasn't all that young anymore, because I was a latecomer, and it did excite me. I adored my mother, I loved my mother.

She used to tell me that I was found and that I was not really their child at all. That they had found me on the back steps wrapped in a cloth embroidered with a seven-corner crown and some kind of aristocratic initials.

PART I: THE BIOGRAPHY

CHAPTER ONE

CHILDHOOD

I WAS BORN one Sunday morning at 11:30 on the 31st of October, 1920, in a neighborhood of Berlin called Schöneberg. My mother told me that it had been raining all day but that when I arrived the sun suddenly came out.

My mother came from a wealthy family and had married a rich man who had died when she was quite young.

They had had one child, my half-brother, Hans. My father came from a poor family that lived in a tiny village in Silesia. When he married my mother, he took over a factory that had belonged to my mother's first husband, which produced buckles and buttons.

My mother was full of fancy and told me wonderful stories about the way she had met my father, Max, and how he had fallen in love with her beautiful legs.

She did have beautiful legs. She was an attractive young widow, and he was a poor soldier not long back from fighting the Russians in 1918. They fell in love and married. I was born during the Allied blockade of Germany after the 1914–18 war, two months premature—a sickly child. There was no cow's milk available, so I was brought up on goat's milk, all you could get in Berlin

at the time. It made me healthy, handsome, and very strong. That was my mother's version of events.

A few years ago, when my wife, June, and I went to Berlin, we visited Joachim, who used to be the family chauffeur. He had recognized me in a German magazine and contacted us. Now, Joachim's wife had for many years been in service with an uncle of mine called Goldschmidt, so she really knew the family history. I think it was through her that Joachim had got the job as chauffeur for my father. So, while June and I were sitting around the table in his little house in the suburbs having coffee and cake, some old family stories came out.

Did you know, Helmut, that you were not born premature at all? I said I didn't know, that I had always believed the story I'd been told and had no reason not to. Indeed, she said, your father courted your mother very intensely, and obviously they must have slept together before they were married, because she was two months pregnant when they went to the altar and got married.

Joachim's wife was adamant that this story was true, and apparently many members of the family were au courant with it. They all knew that it was true love Max and Claire had had for each other, and that they were sleeping with each other long before they married.

Joachim's wife went on to tell us more family stories. The wedding of Uncle Goldschmidt had not been without drama. It appears that when he married my aunt they came out of the synagogue and in the crowd there was a woman waiting with a babe in her arms. As the newly wedded couple came out, this woman held the babe up above the heads of the crowd and screamed, "This is your child! It's your child!"

The Markiewiczes, my mother's side of the family, were rich in bizarre personalities. My mother's father, Grandfather Markiewicz, born in 1844, became a Wanderbursche and crisscrossed the country to seek his fortune; he ended up in Italy, where he tried to join Garibaldi in the war of independence, but was rejected because of his youth. He then sailed to America, and enlisted in the Union Army in 1865. For part of his service he was attached to the special guards of Mrs. Grant, the general's wife. She took a liking to him and sent him to the artillery school at Fort Monroe, Virginia. He became an American citizen, changing his name to Marquis because his mates could not pronounce Markiewicz. He then returned to Berlin, married, and had three sons and five daughters. One of these was my mother, Claire, or Klara.

Grandfather Markiewicz was an advertising pioneer who made a fortune by putting advertisements on public transport—buses and trolleys. His great hobby was his coach and six horses, with which he would traverse Berlin at great speed. The story goes that he loved his horses so much that, when their blankets were worn out and not good enough for them anymore, he would

Geburtsurkunde.

Nr. 827

Berlin-Schöneberg, am 2. November 1920

Vor dem unterzeichneten Standesbeamten erschien heute, der Persönlichkeit nach auf Grund der Bescheinigung seiner Eheschließung aner kannt,

der Kaufmann Max Neustädter,

wohnhaft in Berlin-Schöneberg, Innsbrucker Straße 24,

Religion, und zeigte an, daß von der

Klara Neustädter geborenen Marliewiez, seiner Ehefrau,

Religion,

wohnhaft bei ihm,

zu Berlin-Schöneberg, in seiner Wohnung,

am einunddreissigsten Oktober des Jahres tausend neunhundert zwanzig vor mittags

um elf drei viertel Uhr ein Knabe geboren worden sei und daß das Kind den Vornamen

Helmut

erhalten habe.

Vorgelesen, genehmigt und unterschrieben
Max Neustädter

Der Standesbeamte.

In Vertretung: Huth

Daß vorstehender Auszug mit dem Geburts-Haupt-Register des Standesamts Berlin-Schöneberg

zu

gleichlautend ist, wird hiermit bestätigt.

am 4. Juni 1938

Der Standesbeamte.

In Vertretung

Beglaubigt
Berlin, den 10. Juni 1938
Der Stadtpräsident
Der Reichshauptstadt Berlin
Im Auftrage

give them to the cheapest tailor he could find, and out of those horse blankets would be made his daughters' winter coats.

My mother was a bit of a snob, but this was a common trait of many Berliners. They looked down their noses at those who were not up to the sophistication of the big city. Although Max himself had very quickly taken on the urbane polish of a Berliner, his family had not. My mother despised her in-laws, my father's family. Coming from Silesia, they were by no means chic, and there were far too many of them for her taste. She always complained that Father had too many relatives.

We lived in a building on the Innsbruckerstrasse. At the front door of our building, as on all others on the street, there was a big black bell button, set in a shiny bronze dish, surrounded by an enamel frame on which was written "Aufgang nur für Herrschaften." When someone pressed the bell, a little window above would open and the concierge would poke his head out and examine the caller. If he did not look like a Herrschaft, or gentleman, he would shout at him to use the servants' entrance.

Under the rafters of the roof was what was called the Boden. It ran the whole length of the building and was used by all the maids to do the washing, drying, and ironing of the "grosse Wasche" (sheets, towels, etc.). In between work, the maids used to sing Hintertreppen Moritaten, i.e., "Sabinchen war ein Frauenzimmer, gar treu und lobesam. . . ." I loved going up there: it always smelled good of the fresh laundry, and the white sheets used to move gently in the breeze. Many of my fashion photographs have been taken in places that remind me of my childhood, and these kind of laundries can be found even today in the big old hotels where I like to photograph.

Our apartment was on the third floor of the building, which was shaped like a tower. I would stand on the balcony looking up at the sky to watch the zeppelin come in from America, and I would look down to the street and watch the pitched battles between the cops and communists and Nazis.

There was a green strip with trees down the center of the street. The traffic went up and down on either side, and in the middle the cops would charge with batons, chasing the people, and the people would beat each other up. This was in the early 1930s, before Hitler came to power; six million people were unemployed. The depression pushed people to political extremes, both left and right. My parents were not involved in politics at all. They were totally unpolitical, which was bad in a way for my father's future. The smart German Jews left in 1933 and 1934, but many did not recognize the threat. Though it was spelled out in *Mein Kampf*, nobody had read *Mein Kampf*.

When I was fifteen I said, We've got to leave, this is never going to change.

My family had total financial security, even during the period of incredible inflation. When people got paid, they had to go to collect their salary with a wheelbarrow. The banknotes were so enormous that you couldn't carry the money away.

My brother collected it. At home we had albums full of it.

The apartment was as big as a house. It had about ten rooms, all of which led off the long main hall. At the entrance was a spacious foyer, with a big green tile stove and a large Oriental carpet. It had elaborate parquet floors, as did the rest of the apartment. There was also a big wooden gramophone, which we used a lot. My parents loved to dance. They would roll the carpet back when they were entertaining. I can remember everyone dancing around the vestibule.

The house was furnished with heavy dark furniture. The dining room had a big oak table with turned legs which looked like giant corkscrews. The wood was so dark it was almost black. It would have taken four strong men to lift it. Even the chairs were too heavy for me to move. I had to be pushed into my place at the table. There was a very heavy oak sideboard, against one wall with an enormous grandfather clock opposite it.

We were given spinach to eat, which we hated. Our Kinderfräulein often pinched my cheeks, forcing me to swallow the stuff. We used to throw it into the grandfather clock when her back was turned during lunch. The spinach turned black as it aged, matching the wood. One day, mice were found in the

dining room. Our stash of spinach was discovered, creating a family drama and a confrontation in the Herrenzimmer between my father, Hans, and me.

The Herrenzimmer, translated literally to mean "gentlemen's room," was my father's retreat. It was the smoking room, like a library or study, furnished with big club chairs that had brass ashtrays on weighted suede belts hanging over the arms. There was a big mahogany writing desk and a chandelier. Everything in there was heavy and dark, even darker than in the dining room.

The hired help worked long, hard hours. They were on call twenty-four hours a day. The only time they had off was every Thursday evening and every second Sunday. It was more like slavery than anything else.

I recall my mother leaning out of the window of the apartment, watching a maid leave on her day off, exclaiming, "My God! This girl is dressed as well as I am! She doesn't know her place. I can't have that." And the maid was fired as soon as she returned. My mother just didn't tolerate that kind of thing. Everyone had to know his or her place and stay in it.

I remember one very good-looking East Prussian maid. (A lot of house-maids came from East Prussia to Berlin to work. They were great big girls with great big asses.) In the morning, when she pulled up the blind in my fa-ther's bedroom, my father would lean out of bed, screw his monocle into his eye, and hit her on the ass, saying, "Teufel! Teufel!" ("Devil! Devil!")

I had my own room and a nanny whose only job was to take care of me. I was tremendously spoiled. I had an enormous number of toys and a never-ending supply of new ones. I'd play with them for a few days when they were brand-new, then abandon them, tossing them aside in favor of the even newer ones that arrived regularly. There was nothing that I was denied.

I was insufferable, but I was cute. If I wanted something, I got it—I just badgered my parents until they bought it for me. I recall throwing tantrums until they bought me an expensive toy stagecoach that I wanted. Three days after I got it, I wasn't interested in it anymore. I also remember an elaborate model-train set that gathered a lot of dust. Everyone else's needs were less important than my own. It was almost impossible to get me to do anything I didn't feel like doing.

I had several armies of tin soldiers, which managed to hold my attention for a time. I'd set up complicated battle scenes, aided by my East Prussian grandmother on my father's side, a real soldier's woman who knew all about the army and all about the regiments. She lived not far from us and survived into very old age.

Between meals, the table in the dining room was covered with an Oriental carpet. I remember helping my grandmother roll the cloth off the table so that the two of us could play with my little armies. We used to pore over pic-ture books on German field regiments to work out our battlegrounds. Then she helped me put my tin soldiers into proper battle order. The trouble was that after a day of playing with the soldiers I wouldn't want to look at them again for several weeks. I would stare out the window at the snow and the cold and stamp my feet and scream, "What will I do now? What will I play with next?"

I'm afraid that this kind of lack of concentration has stayed with me right through my life. I get bored very easily, and I think this is one of the reasons why I have never wanted to make movies. A movie is a project that you have to give a lot of time to—many months, sometimes years of your life—and that is something that I have never been able to do. That's why I love photography and always say that any job that will take longer than three days isn't worth doing. Three days is the limit of my attention span.

I had not only toys but a mountain of books as well. I loved Erich Kästner's stories, like *Pünktchen and Anton*, and *Emil and the Detectives*. Uncle Moritz, who lived in Leipzig, was a publisher. I was showered with expensive children's books that he had published. They had red leather covers and gorgeous illustrations. Uncle Moritz sent us everything, including almost every fairy tale you could imagine. There were fables by Aesop and the well-known German author Hauff, as well as Hans Christian Andersen and the Brothers Grimm, and even some Greek mythology, all illustrated in full color.

Some of the illustrations were pretty risqué, at least for a six-year-old. I remember looking at a picture of Cleopatra floating down the Nile with her snake. Her ample bust was covered with a tight-fitting molded copper breastplate. She looked quite voluptuous, wearing a long, diaphanous skirt and reclining on some cushions on her barge. This was a very suggestive image for a young boy.

There was a story in one of my books that absolutely terrified me. It was a tale of beggar thieves who kidnapped the children of rich people. In this story they stole a little boy and bound his legs underneath him so it looked like he didn't have any. Then they sat him on a bridge to beg for money from passersby. They told the little boy he couldn't speak or yell for help or they would do terrible things to him.

I knew there were lots of beggars in the streets of Berlin, and there was one particular bridge that we used a lot. The metro ran underneath it. Every day I went over that bridge, and every day I was scared that somebody would steal me and turn me out to beg for money on that bridge. I imagined seeing my parents go by and not being able to cry out for help. I used to terrify myself by imagining myself in the most frightening situations I had read about.

Another image was even more frightening. It was a picture of a genie in a bottle. Every night I took the book to bed with me and looked at the illustration by flashlight. I was absolutely hypnotized by it. Then I started having nightmares. I was afraid the genie would come out of the bottle and sit on its owner's chest and suffocate him. I was terrified that the genie would crush me to death. Whenever I started to think about it, I psyched myself out. The walls of the nursery seemed to close in on me, and I began screaming hysterically. I begged and pestered my mother to tear the picture out of the book. She didn't want to ruin one of Uncle Moritz's books, but when I didn't stop shrieking she finally removed it.

There's a beautiful term in French for an empty lot—a *terrain vague*. It's someplace where only weeds grow. You find these sometimes in between buildings, but in this particular case, there was a *terrain vague* opposite the apartment building where I was born, and sometimes in the summer a little circus or a sideshow would pull up there.

I used to look out the window and beg my Kinderfräulein to take me down there and let me walk through the booths and look at the fat woman and the sideshows. There was something forbidden about it. I would have to be home by seven. There weren't many freaks, although there were people who showed themselves for money.

Throughout my childhood, my mother harped on about the fact that I was two months early as a way of explaining why I was such a sickly child. I was physically very weak; I don't think I had a muscle in my body. I guess because I was so frail, I was very sheltered. To protect my delicate constitution, my parents were very strict about my going to bed early. On Saturday nights, though, I was allowed to stay up till nine, listening to the radio on a crystal set my parents had given me. I turned it on right after my mother came in and kissed me before going out for the evening.

My parents worried about germs all the time. I was brought up never to touch a banister. I wasn't allowed to handle money. My contact with other children was very limited. I wasn't allowed to play in the sandbox in a public park with other children (I had my own private sandbox). Some of this has stayed with me. I still don't like touching banisters, and I hate being touched by other people. I was a dreadful sissy. I was scared of everything and everybody.

A uniformed chauffeur used to bring me to school and pick me up. Nobody else in the school had a chauffeur.

The kids would wait for me and beat me up, because they knew I wasn't going to defend myself. I used to come home screaming hysterically. It bothered me to be beaten up by other kids and to be the butt of physical jokes. These things didn't happen because I was Jewish, just because I couldn't defend myself.

It didn't help that my mother dressed me like a little girl. I wore velvet suits with high stiff collars—they were called Schiller collars—and enormous taffeta bows. The suits had short pants, which I wore with white stockings and black patent-leather shoes. No one else was dressed that way. On top of it all, my mother kept my hair in a pageboy bob, à la Louise Brooks. I looked like Little Lord Fauntleroy. Whenever I went into a shop, they would look at me across the counter and say, "Ah, hello, little girl!"

I used to faint all the time. At the dinner table, all of a sudden I'd be on the floor, out cold. This happened so often that the family took almost no notice of it. They'd say, "Oh, it's just Helmut. He's fainted again." When I passed

out, my mother would have the nanny dunk my wrists in cold water to revive me. My parents took me to the doctors. They couldn't find anything wrong with me physically and thought I just suffered from nerves, like my mother, who claimed to be a very high-strung woman. She made everybody believe this, but I'm not so sure that she was. I think it was a role that she played very successfully.

She used it, I think, as a means of controlling us. I remember her very theatrically holding the bridge of her nose between her thumb and forefinger and sighing, "Oh my God, my nerves! My nerves!"

During the week, Father would have lunch in town and we would take our midday meal à trois, my mother, my brother, and I.

Hans and I fought terribly, and my mother kept a black book by her side at the table. She would tell us, "I'm much too nervous, boys. I cannot cope with you. I will put everything you say and do into this black book, and when your father comes homes, I will show it to him and he will deal with you." She and her "nerves" were very well organized that way—it was all down in black and white. Nevertheless, we were really scared of that black book.

When she picked me up from school when I was very little, she'd bend down to me and say, "Tell me, Helmut, how do I look today? Do I have many wrinkles?" By that time, of course, I was smart enough to know that it was not wise to say, "Yes, you've got a lot of wrinkles today, Mother," so I'd say, "You look gorgeous, Mother, you haven't got one single wrinkle," and she would be ever so pleased.

I also had very weak ankles. I used to trip along by her side. She'd have me by the hand, and every twenty meters or so, I would trip over something and go over on my ankle, and she would hold her stomach and say, "What are you doing to me? You make me more nervous than ever!" and she would crack me over the head with a big diamond ring that she'd turn into her palm. She was quite something, my mother! She used to say to me, "You're the nail to my coffin, you're the nail to my coffin!"

The apartment on Innsbruckerstrasse was right next to the Schöneberger

Stadtpark. Every day, between two and four in the afternoon, my Kinderfräulein and I were expelled from the house and sent to the park so that my mother could have her nap. No disruption to the routine was tolerated. Her "nerves" absolutely forbade it. We weren't allowed to stay indoors under any circumstances. The slightest noise in the house, the tiniest creak of the floorboards, would send my mother into a fit of hysteria.

Rain or shine, hot or cold, my nanny and I were banished from the house. I hated how my mother pushed us out that way. She didn't give a shit whether I froze to death with my nurse in the park or not. She said she was doing it for my ankles and my health—"It's good for you, my boy, you need fresh air!"—but I thought that she was just being selfish. (Surely I should be the only one in the family who got what I wanted all the time.)

ı the winter she still dressed me only in short pants with a little jacket
long woolen stockings. I froze. To me those daily walks were sheer tor-
ture, nothing more than cruel enforced marches. They are indelibly etched in
my memory. I'm sure this is another reason why I love summer and absolutely despise winter.

Because Hans was ten years older than I was, my early childhood coin-
cided with his teenage years. Hans had a collection of girlie magazines that he
kept locked away in the writing desk in his bedroom. I remember in particular *Das Magazin*, which came out monthly and always had a nude woman in
it. It had a section of beautiful naked models who wore shoes with the little
heels that were the fashion of that period and black silk stockings that were
held up only by what looked liked rubber bands—no garters, no belts. My
parents knew nothing about them, but I knew they were there. I learned how
to pry open the locked drawer in the desk. I would jimmy the drawer, then
take the magazines into the loo and lock myself in, to study them very closely.

My mother had a fetish about constipation. I wasn't allowed to pull the
chain until she had examined the bowl to determine whether I'd shat enough.
It was an obsession. I think it's very German: you must be regular, it's the
bodily equivalent of making trains run on time.

Now, because I was looking at these magazines in the bathroom, I was
spending a lot of time in there. Eventually, my mother became concerned
that I was constipated.

One day, as I was coming out of the bathroom with *Das Magazin* under my
arm, my mother caught me on the way back to my brother's bedroom to return it. "What have you got there, Helmut?" she asked me. I was only six years
old. I had to show her the magazines and confess where they came from.
There was a terrible row; my mother grabbed the magazine and collected all
the other magazines that my brother had kept in the drawer and burned
them. Hans beat me up as punishment, but for me that was nothing new. He
beat me up quite frequently when I was young. Anyway, that was that as far
as *Das Magazin* was concerned.

My parents' obvious preference for me colored my relationship with my brother, Hans, throughout my childhood. He was all too aware of his status as the stepson. His only ally was rich Uncle Edward, my mother's brother, who lived in a beautiful villa in Dahlem. Everyone said that he and Hans looked very much alike. They were very close.

My mother tried to hide her preference for me, but my father did not. He was tough on Hans and never let him forget that he was someone else's son. Even his name was different. His name was Hans Egon Hollander, Hollander being the surname of his father, my mother's first husband. I'm sure that life at home was very difficult for him and that he resented me.

He used to do his best to make me suffer. The fact that I was a spoiled brat

made it that much easier. I remember walking with him one Sunday morning in the Grunewald. I was very little, about five years old. He was fifteen. We came to a big thicket of nettles. He told me, "I'll give you twenty pfennigs if you sit in that bush there." I was wearing shorts. I didn't have any idea what a nettle was, but twenty pfennigs were enticing. So I sat in the nettles and I screamed. The nettles stung my legs, they stung my ass, they went right up my shorts. I was in agony. My mother really let Hans have it when we got back home, which made him resent me even more, and I never got my twenty pfennigs. That's how it was between my brother and me.

In his teenage years, Hans was extremely wild. He hated school and was an even worse student than I was, if that was possible. Three years in a row, he was not promoted into the next class. He was very taken with the exploits of American gangsters. Jack "Legs" Diamond was his particular idol, and Hans sought to imitate him in a number of ways. He bought himself a double-breasted suit with wide lapels and pinstripes and took to wearing flashy brocade vests. He parted his hair in the middle and slicked it down with pomade. For a time, he wore a hair net. He grew a little mustache, like Adolphe Menjou. He really looked like a gangster; my parents were not pleased.

It was not only his clothes. Hans and his friends also had canoes, which were very fashionable in those days. Each of the canoes carried the name of an American gangster. Hans's canoe was of course called *Jack Diamond*; his best friend's was named *Al Capone*. Every weekend, they went out on the Wannsee with their canoes. The canoes had little canvas tops; they even slept in them. I could never figure out how they could fuck in them without turning them over.

When I was about seven, he began running around with a very rough crowd. He had gotten in with a gang of break-in thieves who had been committing burglaries in the Schöneberg neighborhood. When my parents took me away on holiday, he was left home alone with the staff. He tipped his friends off to the fact that the family was gone, and they raided the apartment. My brother even opened the door for them.

When we came back from our trip, Hans had to endure a family inquiry led by my father, who was particularly stern with him, saying that he had betrayed his family and so forth. After the incident he was supervised very closely, so that he didn't associate with people like that again. However, this did not stop him from taking up with young men who were not gangsters but were mainly interested in fucking as many girls as possible.

I remember that he and his friends used to take cars or taxis to the surrounding villages, out in the Lake District. About a dozen guys would go together into the villages and tell the naïve country girls that they were part of a movie company. It was their version of the casting couch: "Lie down, I'm going to make you a star." Of course, the locals didn't know any better, and Hans and his pals fucked them and had a great time.

Hans was also a comedian and a practical joker. He loved to tell Jewish jokes at dinnertime, and he loved speaking Yiddish, which really aggravated my father. He'd just hit the roof. He would slam his fist down on the table and say, "I will not have these jokes and this talk at my table!" He wanted everything to be in German; there was no Yiddish allowed. Since Hans was doing so poorly in school, my father forced him to go into the family business. He absolutely hated it, just as he hated school. He tried very hard to sabotage the business, making fun of the customers and telling them his Jewish jokes. He answered the phone in my father's office in the voice of the actor-comedian Felix Bressart, whom he imitated perfectly. Since the customers had no sense of humor, they didn't appreciate it at all. Neither did my father: all the clients complained to him. There was a great deal of tension at home concerning my brother's future.

In the end, he did achieve his goal and was thrown out by my father, because he did more harm than good in the company. When he was in a good mood and feeling amiable toward me, Hans would sometimes take me for walks. One evening when I was seven, he took me down the Tauentzienstrasse to KaDeWe, a famous department store. There was a woman standing on the street corner. Hans pointed to her and told me, "Have a good look, Helmut. That is the famous Red Erna." Red Erna was a whore who was very well known in that quarter of Berlin, called Red Erna because she had red hair and wore red riding boots and carried a riding whip. This was my introduction to the sinful side of life on the streets of Berlin.

In the Herrenzimmer there was a bookcase with beveled glass doors and green silk curtains on thin brass rods. One section of the bookcase was open and the other section was locked. In the unlocked section were the beautiful books that were gifts from Uncle Moritz. As I learned to read, I became fascinated with the forbidden books that were locked away in the other half of the bookcase. I found the hidden key to this part of the bookcase and soon began smuggling books into bed at night. Instead of using my flashlight to scare myself shitless looking at the picture of the genie in the bottle, I began using it to read the books that I had sneaked out of the library. It was just a small flashlight, which as the batteries grew weaker gave off only the faintest red glimmer. (With my allowance I couldn't afford to keep buying batteries; besides, to do so would have aroused suspicion.) Even though I could barely make out the words on the page, I kept reading. I began to wear glasses at a very early age.

My parents obviously thought I was far too young for such literature, but the books I was reading included wonderful novels such as *Fräulein Else* by Arthur Schnitzler and works by Stefan Zweig. The stories were suggestive but not pornographic. There is a beautiful word in German for it—"schwül"— they were steamy, very erotic, with an enormous amount of sensuality. Nothing was ever spelled out, but they were explicit enough for me to understand what they were all about.

Ever since I was very young, summer has always been my favorite season. It wasn't just the fairs and the sideshows and the coming of the warm weather. I was grateful for the end of school, which I loathed. It was the one thing in my life that I really hated. I was a dreadful student, but I just didn't care. I couldn't wait for the holidays. I always looked forward to going away to the spas on vacation. So did my brother, Hans.

There was a beggar on the Innsbruckerstrasse who played the fiddle. During the summer months, when the well-to-do families left for the seaside, he too packed up his fiddle, and we would find him fiddling away on the promenade of Heringsdorf. Heringsdorf was the preferred seaside resort for Jewish families; Ahlbeck, only a few kilometers away, was full of early Nazis and Stahlhelm followers. The flags flying in Heringsdorf were of the Weimar Republic; in Ahlbeck they were the old colors of the Kaiser or swastikas.

There were many organized amusements for the guests: "Child Beauty Contests" and *concours d'élégance* on such themes as "Madame and her car," "Madame and her dog." All the ladies participating would get dressed up in their most beautiful gowns or beach pajamas. Thaika, my little Pekinese, would be paraded around, and Mother would enter me in the children's beauty contest. Much to the great disappointment of Mother, I never won a prize, because every time I was hauled in front of the judges I would burst into tears and cry hysterically.

In the summer, my parents were forever taking cures. They'd stay in grand hotels, mostly in Germany, where people came to take the cure—the spa water. The women invariably fell in love or had flirtations with the staff of good-looking doctors, who were mostly young men. There was a dining room with a dance floor in the middle. The children and their nannies had their own dining room. A gigolo and a gigolette sat at separate tables away from the customers.

The gigolo would dance with the ladies who came to take the cure on their own, and the gigolette would dance with the gentlemen. We stayed at one place somewhere in the Harz where every Friday night they held an after-dinner dance. There were lampions in the garden of the grand hotel. The dining room was turned into a ballroom. The ladies all dressed up—my mother included—wearing pearls and pretty dresses with lots of flesh showing. I don't think I was more than four years old, wallowing in this grown-up excitement, when a lady in evening dress snatched me up and sat me on her shoulders, holding my arms out with her hands.

Sitting so high, with my penis rubbing against the nape of her neck, I had one of the first erections I remember.

My father was taking the cure in a sanatorium called "Der Weisse Hirsch" in the hills above Dresden. One day Mother decided it would be lovely to give Father a surprise and visit him. So we took the night train from Berlin. My poor mother, suffering with gallstones, had a terrible attack of pain caused by the movement of the train and screamed with pain for a hell of a long time. I, a seven-year-old kid, of course didn't know what to do, and the trip was terrifying for me. Once we pulled into the station, the pain subsided and Mother was back to her normal high-strung condition. We took a taxi up to the sanatorium, drove through the gates, and what do we see on the big lawn in front of the main building but Father and some other middle-aged Berlin businessmen in their black floppy shorts and white singlets throwing a big medicine ball back and forth to three pretty blonde physical-health instructors. The rest of the spa staff was equally handpicked. Well, Mother got Dad dressed, and we were all off together on the train back to Berlin.

Another year, we went to another spa for a cure. There too were the habitual cotillions for the Friday evenings and Saturday nights. Again, a gigolo and a gigolette.

My brother must have been about fifteen or sixteen. He fell madly in love with a gigolette who wore her hair in an Eton crop. I remember our father catching him in the bathroom while the gigolette was stark naked in the bathtub and he was shaving her neck. My father came in and made a terrible scene. It was another big family drama, and then my brother, in order to revenge himself against the family and everybody there, collected a whole lot of very small frogs and put them in the mustard pots on the dining tables. Then he took a number of silver tea eggs after the tea had been served and emptied the sodden wet tea leaves into the hotel's letterbox. It was crammed with postcards waiting to be sent off to friends of the guests who were staying in the hotel. He took me along to observe the postman collecting this shocking, sodden mess from the postbox. It was quite a scene.

I made quite a scene myself during one of these visits to a spa, when I suddenly appeared in front of my mother while she was having afternoon tea in the garden of the hotel with her friends. I had accepted a ride on a horse-drawn night cart and had been invited to sit up front with the driver on a bench with no back. The driver had pulled up suddenly, and I had toppled back into the shit. My mother was filled with grief to have her lovely afternoon tea spoiled by her stinking little son, and I was hauled off to the bathroom.

When the family returned from vacations, the entire household staff would be on hand to greet us. They'd hold a sign saying "Welcome Home," which they could either buy in a stationery store or make themselves. When we came back, the sign had to be up, with the staff standing under it. If it wasn't, my father would be furious. They didn't do this because they particularly loved us. It was just expected. A part of a ritual.

I adored Sundays, when my father used to take me with him down the Grunewaldstrasse for morning drinks with his friends at the Stammtisch. The drinks were called Frühschoppen—eye-openers—but it was really just an excuse for everyone to get together. I loved listening to what they had to say.

I think these Sunday-morning outings were his way of trying to counteract the feminizing influence of my mother. I'm sure as I got older he began to be concerned that his dear son wasn't very masculine, either in action or in appearance. When I was nine years old, he sent me to a gymnastic school for undermuscled, under-everything Jewish kids on Hardenbergstrasse. It was run by two elderly spinster sisters. I hated them. I hated gymnastics. I hated the smell of the sweat of the boys and girls.

We were all about the same age, and we all wore sweatshirts embroidered with the initials "T.G." It was the monogram of the women who ran the gymnastic school, but my mother used to say, "Ah, here come the Tiller Girls!" (The Tiller Girls were a very popular troupe of dancers in the Berlin cabarets.) This of course only made me hate it more.

They made me go twice a week. We had to lie on our backs and put our legs over our heads, keeping our knees straight. My knees were always crooked, because I was knock-kneed, and I remember the woman coming round and pushing my feet down. I invariably used to fart into her face as she bent down to keep my knees straight. She soon gave up trying to keep my knees straight, because the punishment she endured was really pretty heavy. So that's one way I got out of having to become a muscular young man.

My father knew that trying to make a man out of me was going to be a difficult job. I fainted. I fell down all the time. I was scared shitless of everything. I was dressed like a girl. I was a whiny, spoiled brat. I don't think he got much support from my mother—she loved me in my pageboy haircut and my velvet suits.

Finally, when I was twelve, he did the only thing he could think of. Without telling my mother, he took me to a barber and had my hair cut off. She burst into a flood of tears when she saw me. "My God! Where's my pretty little Helmut?" she cried, with tears streaming down her face. The days of velvet suits and pageboy bobs were over. I never thanked my father for doing that, but it changed my life.

CHAPTER TWO

MY APPRENTICE YEARS

BERLIN WAS ALWAYS a city of music. Throughout the twenties and thirties, American jazz bands performed regularly in the clubs and cabarets and were immensely popular. We were mad for jazz. I especially loved Cab Calloway, Jack Hylton, Duke Ellington, and all the Big Bands.

In my teenage years I had a portable gramophone called an Electrola which was stored inside what looked like a little suitcase. It was covered with black leatherette and was my most prized possession. I cut pictures out of magazines and pasted them on the cover.

Inside the lid was a compartment where you kept your 78 rpm records in their brown paper protective sleeves. In the bottom were the speaker and the turntable. On either side of the turntable were little slots where you kept the steel needles. I remember the beautiful little tin boxes the needles came in, with the RCA "his master's voice" dog on the top. The needles didn't last long. I used them to the very last, when they were scratchy and blunt. I even remember using my thumbnail when I ran out of needles and had no more money to buy new ones.

I played my music at full volume all hours of the day or night. My mother would come into my room and ask me why I wasn't playing "The Blue Danube."

I was given piano lessons until one day the teacher put his hand up my short pants, which sent me screaming out of the room, never to return. This my mother wholeheartedly condoned, having a horror that her little Helmie would turn homosexual.

My parents believed that it was important to learn all the social graces, including ballroom dancing. For generations, every prosperous Jewish family had sent their children to a particular dancing school. My brother had gone there as a kid, and at the age of twelve I was enrolled as well. The sessions were held on Saturdays, late in the afternoon.

My friends and I began to play hooky and would skip out to the bars along the Tauentzienstrasse. All the housemaids would be in there dancing. There were some whores as well. My friends and I felt very smart and adventurous. We used to light up cigarettes, hold them elegantly between two fingers, then ask these girls for dances. We only did it to get a hard-on and try to rub ourselves off against them.

That's how I learned to dance. Not surprisingly, I never became very good at it.

So I could practice my dancing, my mother would take me to the five o'clock tea dances on the roof garden of the Eden Hotel, near the zoo. I loved going with her as an escort. I still remember the Art Deco marquee on the façade of the hotel. It was elegant and glamorous and epitomized all that I loved about the city of Berlin. I loved going into the Underground, and I loved traveling on top of the bus and looking down at the street. It was a great city to grow up in.

Photography in Berlin was truly exciting at the time. I'd always been intrigued by my father's camera. It was a big Kodak model that folded out, called an Etui. It was covered in leather, with an optical-exposure meter.

You looked through a hole at a blue light which told you after many complicated reckonings what the exposure would be at the moment you wanted to take your picture. You practically had to be a mathematician to snap the shutter. It made big negatives of an odd size. He took some good photographs, including most of the pictures of my mother and me when I was little.

I of course was never permitted to use it. Shortly after my haircut, however, in 1932, I bought my first camera, at a store called EPA, which was a German version of Woolworth's, when I was twelve years old, with my pocket money. It was an Afga Tengor Box. I immediately decided to shoot the first roll of film (eight pictures, 6 X 9 cm) in the Berlin metro. I emerged from

the metro in Witzleben Station. I had one frame left on my roll. In front of
me, outside the station, stood the Berlin radio tower, the Funk Turm. I tilted
my camera up to the tower in a slightly diagonal angle, no doubt influenced
by Moholy-Nagy, and pushed the trigger. When I picked up my film from the
corner drugstore, there were seven blanks (the photos taken in the metro)
and number eight showed a somewhat fuzzy image of the Funk Turm. I
thought it was a remarkably good shot and knew I was launched on a great
career as a photographer. The original was lost during my many travels as a
young man.

My father garaged his car, the Essex Super Six, around the corner from
our house. There were a number of spaces, and in one of them there was a
gorgeous open white American tower—was it a Cord, belonging to the great
photographer Munkacsi? I was already besotted with photography and would

hide in a corner of the garage waiting for Munkacsi to drive in, park his car, haul lots of cameras out of the backseat, and disappear into the street. I admired his pictures that were regularly published in the *Berliner Illustrirte* which was delivered every week with lots of other magazines to our apartment. I could see myself as the "Rasende Reporter" traveling all over the world, flashing my press pass, which would give me entry into the most glamorous places. It was 1933 and I was thirteen.

Already an avid reader, I now dived into books and magazines on photography. I scoured the news kiosks of Berlin for material. I consumed photographic magazines like the *Berliner Illustrirte* and my brother's old favorite, *Das Magazin*. Like a sponge I soaked up all the images that were in those magazines. I remember being particularly impressed with a photo by Heinz von Perckhammer of some beautiful blonde girls sitting in a BMW. They were called genre photographs. I was hooked.

I was also hooked on sex, or at least the possibility of sex. I got my first French kiss from the daughter of the concierge on Innsbruckerstrasse. We were playing blindman's buff at a party. (In German we called it "blind cow.") All the lights were out and the heavy curtains were drawn. She just put her tongue in my mouth, and it absolutely rocked me.

On October 31, 1933, I celebrated my thirteenth birthday. In most Jewish households, this would be the time for a boy's Bar Mitzvah. Not in ours. I was not Bar Mitzvahed. Neither was Hans. My mother told me I couldn't have a Bar Mitzvah because Hans hadn't had one—it wouldn't have been fair. I was circumcised. Hans never was. We were very unreligious. My father took me to the synagogue two or three times a year. My mother never went at all. She refused. I wasn't interested in religion either. I thought it was a total bore.

We didn't celebrate many of the Jewish holidays. We didn't keep Hanukkah. In fact, we celebrated Christmas, with a real Christmas tree. We exchanged gifts on Christmas Eve, which in Germany is more important than Christmas Day. It wasn't a social time, it was very family-oriented. We visited relatives, not only my father's all-too-numerous relatives, but my mother's family as well.

I had a cousin on my mother's side whose name was Bennett Wissman. He looked like ten Yids but was only half Jewish. He was a cameraman at the Tobis Film Company. As I got deeper into photography, Bennett encouraged me and helped me a lot. I must have come across some of Brassaï's photos; he was the great master of night photography. All of a sudden I got an urge to photograph Berlin at night, but I wasn't allowed out after dark by myself. Going out at night was out of the question until Bennett came to my rescue and volunteered to accompany me as I took pictures of street scenes at night. We went all over Berlin. I still remember how beautiful the city looked at dusk as the gaslights came on and cars and their headlights streaked by.

I just love dusk. June, my wife, comes into my office at home and says, "How can you sit there? it's almost night." I love dusk because of the mysteriousness of the lights going on very slowly here and there. June loves dawn but she hates dusk, she finds it depressing. I sit until it gets really dark and I can't see anything.

I liked Cousin Bennett for another reason. After our outings, we would gather round the table for a Kaffeeklatsch. Mother, Father, me, Bennett, and Bennett's wife, Elsa, would sip coffee and eat pastries. Elsa was a champion ice-skater who skated professionally in the ice shows. She was totally Aryan, and I have no idea how the hell she fitted into the Jewish part of the family. She used to play with me under the Kaffeeklatsch table and give me a major hard-on.

At the age of ten I had left the Volkschule, or grammar school. From that time on I attended the Heinrich von Treitschke Real Gymnasium, on Prinzregentenstrasse, which had a reputation as a strongly pro-Nazi school.

The Gymnasium was for boys only. Around the corner from the house on Innsbruckerstrasse was the girls' lyceum. We used to look through the fence and watch the girls play handball. We watched their breasts bounce up and down under their thin athletic uniforms.

I was still taking gymnastics lessons twice a week from the spinster sisters. My knees were still bent, and I was still farting in their faces. My father finally acknowledged that gymnastics was never going to be my sport. There remained, however, the problem of how to make his son more manly and physically fit. When I was thirteen, he registered me at the Halenseeschwimmbad for swimming lessons.

I had to be pushed into the pool and I screamed bloody murder, but I learned to swim. I became terribly good at it. I joined a club called BSC—Berliner Schwimm Club. I soon received my Death Skull Certificate for swimming three hours straight. I began to develop a swimmer's body, sleek and lean, with powerful shoulders. I liked the way I looked. I loved the feel of the water. It was an element I felt entirely at home in. Swimming became a passion.

It wasn't just the swimming that attracted me. There were, of course, girls on the swim team. They had great bodies too. There is always a great roundness, a great beauty to a swimmer's body. Swimmers are not stringy and sinewy like bodybuilders who lift weights, because their muscles are always relaxed. Everything is smooth, like a dolphin. I've loved photographing swimmers ever since.

In those days the girls wore regulation black racing suits that were not revealing at all. That didn't stop them from being seductive. The suits were made of thin wool, which clung to the girls' bodies and dried very slowly. Because the suits stayed wet for a long time—particularly across the chest, where there was an extra thickness of wool—the girls' nipples would stay erect. It was the forerunner of the wet T-shirt.

I was still a virgin, but I was masturbating like mad. It was a great pastime that I enjoyed thoroughly. My parents knew what was happening; the stiff bedsheets were impossible to conceal.

In some countries adolescent boys used to be advised that jerking off would make hair grow on their palms. At that time in Germany we were informed that excessive masturbation produced dark circles under the eyes. I used to look at myself in the mirror in the morning, see the deep-purple rings under my eyes, and realize that the whole world was going to know that I'd been beating the flesh.

At first I was very self-conscious about it, but after a while I didn't give a shit. It bothered my mother, though. Eventually, she told me she wanted me to see a doctor about it. She sent me to the family physician, Dr. Ballin.

Dr. Ballin was not a prude. Far from it. He sat me down and gave me the most astonishing lecture. "Now, my boy, I've already talked to your parents, and they've asked me to have a chat with you. I'd rather have you make 'boom-boom' with a girl than masturbate. It's much better for you and a lot more fun. I think it's time you got yourself a girlfriend so you can make 'boom-boom.'" That was what he called it. He didn't say the word "fuck" or anything like that, but his meaning was unmistakable.

Rings under the eyes are still a big thing for me in my work. Generally when you work with models they use makeup to take the little bags away. I always say to the makeup artist (this has been going on for years), "Don't take the masturbation rings away!" and when they don't have any, I'll say, "I'd like some dark masturbation rings under the eyes, please—makes it more interesting!" By now the makeup artists are used to it, because I work very closely with them.

That summer I met some newspaper photographers who lived near our Innsbruckerstrasse apartment. The two men were working in a flat where they had set up a darkroom. They had files of newspaper stories and would go out and shoot a series of photographs to go with them. They sold their photos and stories to a number of German magazines. When I told them how crazy I was about photography, they offered me a job running errands for them.

For me it was a heaven-sent opportunity. I made coffee, filed stories and negatives, and went out for film and supplies. I didn't breathe a word about it to my parents.

In 1934, when I was almost fourteen, we moved from Innsbruckerstrasse to Friedrichsruherstrasse, a beautiful tree-lined street in one of the swanky districts of Berlin. I was delighted because it was just minutes away from the Halenseeschwimmbad. It made going for my workouts easy.

The apartment was on two stories. My room and the kitchen were in the basement, and there was a dumbwaiter that used to bring food up to the dining room. I also used it to haul Thaika upstairs. He always used to be shit-scared, that poor little doggie, and I'd take him out of the dumbwaiter in the dining room trembling like mad.

My poor Thaika had to endure other humiliations. My father used to take me to the Circus Kronc or Sarasani whenever it was in town. I loved the lions and their lion tamers, though they would frighten the shit out of me; that did not stop me once I was back home from making a whip out of a stick and string and cracking it at poor Thaika while yelling, "Come on, Sonja, jump!!" One of the lions in the Sarasani circus was called Sonja, and the ringmaster would call it by its name to make it jump through the hoops.

My room had formerly been the maid's quarters and had a private entrance. My parents wanted me to have privacy. They never came into my room unannounced. Compared with the sheltered existence that I had led as a small child, totally protected by my mother and my Kinderfräulein, I was now granted a surprising amount of independence.

In 1934 the Nuremberg racial laws were drafted. They were extremely complicated and were, amongst other things, designed to separate the Jews from the Aryans. My father was so incensed by this that he had me transferred from the Heinrich von Treitschke Gymnasium to the American School of

Berlin. The reason was that the Jewish pupils at the Gymnasium and in every other German school had been separated from the so-called Aryan students. In my class, we had never had any great problems between Jews and non-Jews, even though many of my schoolmates were in the Hitler Youth.

They had all known that I was Jewish and which of the other guys in the class were Jewish. There had not been much animosity between us; on the contrary, we had got on very well. We'd already known each other for four years. So what the school principals did was to put us Jews in the back of the classrooms, and consequently the network that had been worked out over the years of one guy helping another broke down completely. The Jewish pupils were often smarter than the "Aryans," so the cheating system collapsed.

My father thought all this was going too far. He was still sure that one day the whole thing was going to stop, that Hitler couldn't last. He was one of those Jews who were more German than the Germans. Iron Cross first class, service in the German Army during the 1914–18 war and all that.

My own feelings were quite different. I was pretty much awake to it but didn't give a shit one way or the other.

I regretted that my old man had me transferred, because the American School, down at the American Church of Berlin, on Nollendorfplatz, taught only in English.

For a kid of fourteen suddenly to have to start learning mathematics, algebra, history, and every other subject in English was a nightmare.

My English was almost nonexistent, so I started to go only to American and English movies. On the number 19 bus going down the Kurfürstendamm on my way to school at the Nollendorfplatz I invariably carried the *Times* under my arm to make it look as if I were either American or English.

Usually it was out of date by about three weeks, because I couldn't afford to buy a new paper every day with my pocket money, but still I carried the *Times* and I read it, hoping that everybody in the bus would look at me and admire this gorgeous American kid.

I even tried to dress like an Englishman. It was the fashion of the time. The idea was to look as English or American as possible. You didn't want to look German—that was the last thing you wanted. I spent hours in front of the mirror trying out different looks. Should I wear a tie? How big should the knot be? Should I have my collar up or down? The big decision was whether to wear the sweater outside the trousers or tucked in.

I drove my parents crazy. My mother would yell at me, "Helmut! It's enough. Get away from that mirror!" My apparel of choice became pearl-gray flannels with deep cuffs, an overcoat with a big collar worn turned up, a shirt, a sweater, and a tie. My brother at this age wanted to look like "Legs" Diamond; I looked very *Brideshead Revisited*.

There were no Jewish maids in those days, and it became a problem, as we were only allowed to employ an Aryan housemaid or cook if she was over fifty years old and was not a live-in maid. I reckon the guys who drafted those Nuremberg racial laws thought, Any shiksa over fifty years old, not even a Jew would want to fuck her!

So those glorious days when my father would lean out of bed and smack a Dreitaller girl from East Prussia on the rump were over.

At fourteen, I had my first love affair. I had fallen in love with a champion from my swimming club, a girl called Illa. She was a great swimmer, and we badly wanted to make love, but we didn't know how to. So Illa went to a swimming meet in Breslau one weekend to compete against another club and she said, "Helmut, when I get there, I'll find myself a boy and I'll find out how to do it."

She came back to Berlin on a Saturday. It was mostly weekends that we met. She told me, "I know how to do it, and I'll show you." Illa and I went to my room and locked the door, and she showed me how to make love. After that, she went home to her family and I went into the kitchen. My mother was preparing some food. I was ravenous. I'd just had the first fuck of my life, and I was glowing with excitement, but I was simply starving.

I asked my mother to make me a sandwich, and while I was wolfing it

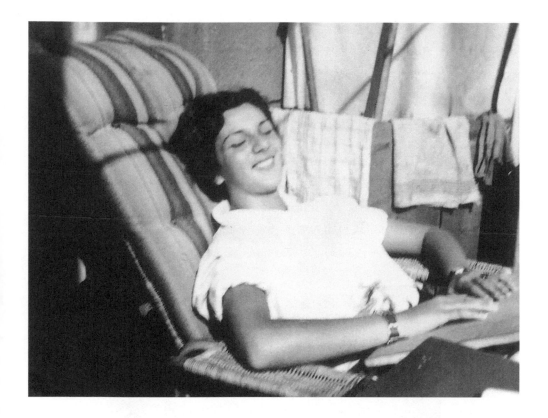

down I told her what had happened. I had no secrets from her whatsoever. I wasn't the least bit self-conscious about telling her about it. After all, I was following doctor's orders.

She said "Helmut, I'm glad you told me, but now you must only do it once a week, because it is very bad for your schoolwork. I will increase your pocket money so that you can buy yourself some condoms, because I don't want you bringing any stuffed pigeons home."

In those days the clap was pretty rampant and syphilis was around too, but above all everybody seemed to get the clap. My brother caught it three times, and the cure in those days was mercury, which was horribly painful. He had to inject his penis with it, and I can remember him screaming in the bathroom, it hurt so much. My mother was wonderful about all that. My father was shy and left all these matters to her.

She explained all the problems of venereal disease and about not getting a girl pregnant and she said, "You know, if you catch something, rather than tell us and be embarrassed, just go to the family doctor and tell him what you have. We will pay the bill, and that way you will feel more relaxed about the whole thing."

I never got the clap, but not because I was particularly careful. Maybe it was because of the company I kept. I wasn't fucking whores or anyone from the wrong side of the tracks. My friends and I were all sleeping with girls from our own social class—girls from well-to-do Jewish families. We weren't interested in drugs or alcohol. We were only interested in girls.

One bright day in 1934, signs went up in cafés all over Berlin—"No Jews or Dogs Allowed."

When I returned to Berlin in the 1950s, I visited the cafés I used to go to: Mampe's on the Kurfürstendamm, and Hardtke's, where the waiters still looked as though they were running concentration camps. The plaques were gone, but their imprints were still there on the walls of Hardtke's.

This sign, "No Jews or Dogs Allowed," also went up at the Halenseeschwimmbad, but I didn't give a shit. I just went on swimming. I ignored the signs and kept up with my two-kilometers-a-day workouts.

There were yellow benches for Jews in the parks and on the streets. The *Stürmer* newspaper was hung in display cases all over town—the whole newspaper, every page. Strangely enough, when the foreigners came to visit Berlin in 1936 for the Olympic Games, the yellow benches, *Stürmer*, and all other outward signs of anti-Semitism disappeared.

In 1935, the American School moved from Nollendorfplatz to a refurbished old villa in Königsallee. This was a godsend for me, because it was just ten minutes from the Halenseeschwimmbad. I began training in earnest. Every morning before school, I walked down Friedrichsruherstrasse to the Halensee, swam a kilometer, jumped into my clothes, grabbed my bookbag, and raced to school. I slid into my seat at the bell, soaking wet. After school I'd work for the photographers and swim another kilometer.

All my training paid off. I became a champion swimmer—not quite Olympic-class, but not far off it. I was very fast over short stretches, like one hundred meters. I was a sprinter. My limited attention span wouldn't tolerate the longer distances.

There was a raft you could swim to at the Halensee, and I remember swimming out there that summer with one of my girlfriends. It was hot, and I planned to fuck her under the water as we hung on to the raft.

I was starting to take her bathing suit off when the Bademeister, or lifeguard, came along. He caught me taking off her suit and banned me from the pool for the rest of the season. That would have been the worst thing that could have happened to me, except that I sneaked back in and continued training and being with my girlfriends.

One day, on my way to the American School on the number 19 bus, I saw a very good-looking girl. She was about twenty-one and I was about fourteen.

I'd see her every morning, and I would look at this girl and the girl would look at me, but, as I was not terribly forward, it took quite a few trips on the bus to school before I worked up enough courage to talk to her.

Like all Berlin kids in the summer, I wore shorts and socks. I remember when I sat down in the bus I used to put my schoolbag and the *Times* across my lap, because, what with the movement of the bus and looking at this much older girl (she must have been a head taller than me), I used to get a hard-on.

I was terribly embarrassed, especially in those short shorts. When my stop came, I'd clutch my schoolbag and newspaper tightly to my crotch and have to mince and hop out of the bus so as not to show my erection.

When I finally plucked up enough courage to talk to this girl, it turned out she was a model in one of the ready-to-wear clothing factories in downtown Berlin. I fell madly in love with this mannequin on the bus. We made clandestine appointments in the corner of the big garden at my apartment. We would meet at six o'clock in the afternoon in the summer and have hot clutching sessions behind the bushes. We kissed like mad. I don't remember whether we actually fucked, but I do remember that it was one of the most exciting romances that I had as a young man.

A few months later, I had a terrible cold and was stuck in bed. My parents, of course, knew nothing of my affair, because I kept it a secret. I was extremely aware of the dangers of a relationship with an Aryan girl. I was laid up in bed for about two weeks, and when the girl rang, I was too scared to admit anything to my parents. In the end, after she had sent flowers and a couple of presents, I had to confess.

My father, who had never, ever maltreated me, had never, ever hit me, gave me two blows behind the ears that were really pretty strong and said, "How could you do a thing like that? You don't know the danger you run!"

He was quite right—the whole family could have ended up in a concentration camp—but when you're fourteen years old and you're in love, what do you do? Whatever it is, you certainly don't think about Nuremberg racial laws!

I promised, I swore, I prayed, I went down on my knees apologizing to my parents, saying that I would never, ever see this girl again . . . but of course I did see her a few more times, until it became really much too dangerous.

· · ·

ONE SATURDAY afternoon at the end of June, I was returning from a photography course. It was not long after we had moved into the new apartment on Friedrichsruherstrasse. I arrived at the Halensee metro station, which was on an elevated platform.

As I got off the train, I spotted a small detachment of young Brown Shirts—storm troopers—at the Halensee bridge, near the entrance to the station. They were members of the radical Nazi militia, the Sturmabteilung, or SA. To get off the platform and head for home, I had to walk past them, which made me very uneasy. However, there was no other way out. As I went by the storm troopers, I remember seeing one face in the front row. Our eyes locked. He was not much older than I was, and he looked just as frightened.

Many years later, in Australia, there was a guy delivered to Tatura Internment Camp that I was in for two years or more with a new lot of detainees. I said, "I've seen you somewhere before. I saw you one Saturday afternoon with your detachment of storm troopers on the Halensee station," and he said, "Yes, you are right. That Saturday afternoon, I left, I fled to London to escape 'the night of the long knives.' " It was June 1934.

AT THE AGE of fifteen, there were just three things in my life: photography, girls, and swimming. My schedule left little time for schoolwork. In October, my father received my report card. It was a disaster. It stated very simply that if I didn't pull my socks up and get down to work at school, I would be expelled. This was shocking, because the American School was a private school and a very expensive one at that. For any student to be so bad that they would consider throwing him out and losing a paying customer was absolutely unheard of. My father had a fit.

I was given a crammer teacher, a tutor. All my cameras were locked away, and I confessed that I had spent my afternoons with those two photographers for months on end instead of doing my homework. I didn't need any help with English, which I'd become pretty good at. I was also good at German, but I could not abide French, mathematics, and history. My tutor was a dreadful woman named Fräulein Salinger. She had ugly gray-black hair that she wore in a fat bun fastened to her head with big bobby pins. She had dandruff, and while she was trying to cram me full of mathematics and French, she used to take one of those big bobby pins out of her hair and start scratching her scalp. When she did that, dandruff would fall like snow all over my desk and my papers.

It was disgusting. Fräulein Salinger, the crammer, came every afternoon. Instead of going to the photographers', I was stuck sitting opposite Fräulein Salinger scratching her fucking scalp and trying to teach me French.

It was no use. I hated school, not the American School in particular, just the fact of school itself. After enduring Fräulein Salinger and her Schuppen as long as I could, I decided on a path of passive resistance. I decided not to do any work at all. What could they do to me? They couldn't beat me. They couldn't make me do it.

If you do not take your baccalaureate, or Abitur in German, the earliest you can leave school is at the age of sixteen. My campaign of passive resistance was a great success. My father despaired of my academic career. My mother, who supported me in my artistic leanings, helped to convince my father to let me quit school on my sixteenth birthday. I wanted out and I got out.

I wanted to become a movie cameraman, like my cousin Bennett. My mother had a family connection with the director Alexander Korda, and I was offered an apprenticeship with him in London. My father had another fit. All our begging and pleading were to no avail. He absolutely forbade me to go. He said that no son of his would ever go into the movie business. To him that was as bad as becoming a waiter, a whore, or a pimp.

My mother turned to me and said, "All right, what do you want to do?" I told her, "If I can't become a movie cameraman, I want to become a photographer." This still didn't please my father. He said, "My boy, you'll end up in the gutter. All you think of is girls and photos."

An education had been designed for young Jews to prepare them for emigration. Even professional people—doctors, lawyers, architects—were learning to be carpenters, printers, and machinists. Here were middle-aged academics and businessmen trying desperately to learn how to make a living with their hands, knowing it might be the difference between life and death.

My father was typical of many of them. In Germany, he was the biggest button-manufacturer in the country, but the only thing he knew how to do was sell fucking buttons. He spoke only German. In a foreign country he was absolutely unemployable.

Later on, when I was in Australia, I knew some people who were much older than me—people who were in their fifties during the war. These people were professors in dentistry, in medicine, who had even written textbooks in German, but whose degrees were not recognized under the Australian laws. They had to retake their examinations and their doctorates in English. These were people whose books had been translated into English. For a person like that, it was very difficult to survive in a foreign country. I am talking about my father's generation, I'm not talking about a kid like me. They couldn't speak any French or any English. English was more important than French, because although a lot of people did go to France it was a very dangerous place to be, because France's record of sheltering Jews was very bad.

Cousin Bennett was more fortunate than many—he still had a job. A lot of firms were being pressured to fire their Jewish workers. Because he was only half Jewish, Bennett was allowed to keep his position at the Tobis Film Company. He did, however, have to become a paying member of the SS. Mercifully, he didn't have to wear a uniform.

So that is why my brother's dream of becoming a farmer had been granted by my father: he could see that there was no other future for Hans. Hans had gone to a farm not far from Berlin and started his education as a farmer. From there he had gone to Denmark. In the summer of 1934, my parents allowed me to visit my brother in Denmark, where he was studying to be a farmer, all by myself. I thought I was very grown-up.

My parents took me to the train station and put me on the train for Copenhagen. I bought myself a pack of Camels and smoked a few in the corridor of the train. I felt incredibly sophisticated, until my brother was late meeting me at the station. Then I was scared shitless. I was almost fourteen years old and I was in a foreign country. I wasn't smoking anymore, I was just standing there shitting myself.

Once Hans finally arrived, however, we got along very well. All the old animosities were gone. He already spoke very good Danish. He lived in the country just outside Copenhagen.

I thought all the girls were beautiful, and I developed a huge crush on the local clergyman's daughter. Hans seemed very happy, but for the life of me I couldn't understand why he wanted to be a farmer.

In 1936 Hans left Denmark for Argentina. He acquired a contract with a Danish farmer outside Buenos Aires and fell in love with the farmer's daughter. When she married him, the father threw them both out of the house. My brother was baptized and became a Protestant. Eventually, he and his wife would be taken back into her family.

ONCE THE Nuremberg laws were in place, my father was not allowed to run his business anymore. They put in a man, an Aryan, who became general director, and my father was reduced to a secondary position. I know he suffered terribly.

I remember coming home late one evening and seeing my father sitting in the study, terribly worried. Even at that age I knew exactly what he was feeling and thinking. I was very fond of him, I loved him dearly. He would sit by himself, because my mother couldn't bear the cigar smoke, and smoke one cigar after another—those big cigars that were put into cardboard cigar-holders. He sat and smoked and played patience; he was very lonely. He didn't know which way to turn. He had totally lost control of the business.

He was merely a figurehead. He would look at me when I came into the room before going to bed, and I could see his heart was broken.

All the money was gone. There was no future, and he was not equipped in any way as a German Jew, as more of a German than a Jew, to deal with the present or the future. Although I was only fifteen when my father's job changed, I knew exactly what was happening. I tried to talk to him. I said, "Father, we must leave, we must, there's nothing we can do here." He said, "But we can't leave, my dear boy, it is impossible, and you have no profession, no craft, how would you survive? We have no money to sustain you abroad." I was too young, I couldn't possibly leave alone; I had to hang on and gain some kind of knowledge that would keep the wolf from the door in the outside world.

Through her connections, my mother got me an apprenticeship with a well-known Berlin photographer named Yva. There was a lot of resistance from my father, but my mother continued to be very supportive and eventually brought him around. In those days, a photography apprenticeship was a state-organized thing. It was like becoming a carpenter or a plumber—you had to serve your apprenticeship, after which you got a certificate. You were not allowed to call yourself a photographer without one. The parents of an apprentice had to pay money to the master photographer. It was a good system, because it meant that you didn't just sweep the floors. The master had a duty to teach the young apprentice his craft.

Yva's real name was Frau Simon. I thought her husband, Alfred Simon, was a total idiot. He was the studio's business manager. Yva did fashion photography, as well as portraits of ballet dancers, actors, and actresses. We did a lot of underwear catalogues, which I loved.

Yva was a good-looking woman. She must have been about thirty-six in those days. I was one of two young assistants. There was another boy, whose name I've forgotten.

These were the happiest days of my youth in Berlin. Yva had a gorgeous studio at number 45 Schluterstrasse. In the two years I was under her tute-

lage I fell madly in love with her. I worshipped the ground she walked on. I adored her photographs. Also, there was a girl, a printer in the darkroom, who was an ex–Bauhaus student. She used to wear black velvet suits with a white shirt and collar. She also wore a monocle—that just drove me sexually insane.

This was 1936; I was sixteen and she was twenty-two. In those days there was a red light in the darkroom. I used to find any excuse I could to get in there, to bring her things or just to look at her. I never missed an opportunity. I still have a penchant for monocles—I adore girls with monocles.

My father wore one, and it had always impressed me, but he never wore a string on his. He used to screw it into his eye, and then, when he lifted his eyebrow, he'd open his waistcoat pocket and let it drop straight into the pocket, just like a golfer.

I've had a monocle in my camera bag for years and years, and whenever I can use it, I do. A number of photographs feature girls wearing monocles. There's one photograph of Paloma Picasso taken in the late 1970s or early '80s in Nice. I hauled out that monocle and said, "Quick, Paloma, put this in your eye." She put it in her eye and I took a quick picture. It really had nothing to do with Paloma, but I've always loved that picture. It became a poster and a postcard, and it is in my *Portraits* book. Paloma always hated the picture and begged me not to use it. I wanted it to be the cover of the first *Helmut Newton's Illustrated* but I couldn't do that to her, it wouldn't have been nice.

In the studio, Yva functioned like a movie director. The assistants set up the shots but she took the photographs. One of my jobs was to summon Frau Yva when preparations were complete. It was a very formal process. When the assistants gave me the word, I would run down the massive corridor, knock on her office door, and say, "Frau Yva, we are ready for you."

She'd follow me to the studio, look through the lens, and say, "Change this, change that, then call me when it's ready," and return to her office. After the adjustments were made, I ran and knocked on her door again. Yva would check the shot, then squeeze the rubber ball, which is how you operated the shutter on the large studio cameras. Then the first assistant would turn the plate around, and she'd squeeze the ball again.

Apprentices had to learn to do everything. I learned how to print and how to retouch a negative. I also learned how to develop film.

The negatives were very big plate films, 18 X 24 cm, that went into stainless-steel hangers suspended in great big development tanks. It was one of my jobs to mix the developer every Monday morning.

It was not ready-made in a can, like we have today, but all the chemicals were delivered in big brown bags and had to be weighed and properly mixed in hot water. It stank like hell. It was quite an intricate process to mix the developer for the week and to replenish it as well.

That first summer, we were photographing in the studio under very hot lights, shooting a catalogue for a fur company. Just like today, all the winter clothes were photographed in the middle of summer. After the session, I had at least fifty negatives to develop.

I went into the darkroom and started processing these big plates. Just above the developing tank were the light switches. There was a red light for orthochromatic films, and there was a regular white-light switch. I was dripping with sweat. There was no air-conditioning, no ventilation. I opened the big tank that held the films on the hangers, took them out to check them, and switched on what I thought was the red light. I hit the white light instead. I quickly shoved everything back into the tank and slammed the lid down, but I knew it was too late. I was so petrified I didn't say anything.

At the end of the day, Yva said, "Helmut, let me look at the negatives you processed this afternoon." I went with her, shivering and shaking like a leaf. I followed her into the darkroom, where the hangers were now suspended in the wash tank. She pulled them out one after another and held them up to the light. They were all fogged. She looked at me and said, "Mein Gott im Himmel! What happened, Helmut?" "I don't know, I don't know!" I lied. "Frau Yva, it's not my fault. Maybe the plate holders leaked light." Of course she knew jolly well it was me who had fogged the negatives, but she didn't say anything else.

Years later, in Melbourne, June and I had a little darkroom that we referred to as "Little Hell" which was just for developing films. I had an assistant, a young boy who was just as green as I was when I was an assistant for Yva.

His job was to load the plate holders for my Graflex. Anyway, he loaded plate holders and I went out to photograph some swimsuits on St. Kilda Beach with my 4 X 5 Graflex Super D. I still have it to this day, it's a truly wonderful camera. Anyway, I go out onto St. Kilda Beach, take the photographs, and come back. I say to my assistant, "Here, develop these." So he develops them and he calls me and he says, "Helmut, what's happened? There are handbags on the film." I replied, "Handbags?" and he said, "Yes, handbags!"

The week before, we had done a handbag catalogue, and there were still some old negatives lying around in the darkroom. This boy, instead of loading fresh film into my plate holders, had loaded the old exposed negatives from the catalogue from the week before. My bathing suits were all photographed onto the old negatives with the bloody handbags on them! So I guess that's a story that must happen to every photographer.

Every Thursday evening, Yva would let us use the studio after office hours to photograph our friends, to practice, and to do whatever we wanted. I dragged in everyone I knew. I took pictures of my girlfriends dressed in my mother's clothes and hats. She of course had all the fashion magazines in those days. There was *Silberspiegel*, *Die Dame*, and German *Vogue*. I imitated the photos that I saw. I was already pretty hot stuff with a camera. I wanted to be a *Vogue* photographer.

I took photos of my pals as well. One of my friends, who was a bit older than I was, was terribly handsome. His name was Peter Kaiser, and I did a number of portraits of him. One was particularly good. His face was tilted up toward the heavens. I put oil on him and spritzed him with water drops to show sweat. It was a very fascist portrait; it suited Peter perfectly, but it was also simply the style of photography in the 1930s. The pictures from the '36 Olympics were all of the noble Aryan, the triumphant German sports hero, still glistening after his tremendous effort and his great victory.

Peter had a friend named Koslowsky who came from an old Prussian family, very Aryan. Koslowsky too wore a monocle. Peter, who was by then dating a girlfriend of my current flame, brought Koslowsky to my seventeenth-birthday party. We rolled the big carpet back in the apartment on Friedrichsruherstrasse and played jazz nonstop on the Electrola. Everyone was having a grand time until my father came in and saw the beginning of a homosexual encounter between Peter and Koslowsky.

Homosexuality was very common in Berlin, but my father was shocked to see it in his own home. He confronted Koslowsky, then threw him out of the house.

Years later, my path was to cross with Koslowsky's and Peter's in Australia, under very strange and different circumstances.

After about six months, Yva called my mother in and said, "Listen, Helmut's doing so well, you don't have to pay any more apprenticeship money. As a matter of fact, to show our appreciation, we will give him a small amount of pocket money." That was wonderful. I was so excited and terribly pleased.

I still went to the Halensee, but on the weekends we all took the tram together out to a big lake called the Wannsee, where Hans used to keep his canoe. The Wannsee had a real beach with sand brought in from the Baltic Sea. About a hundred meters from the beach there was an artificial island anchored in the lake called the Juvena Insel (island). Juvena was and still is the name of a swimsuit manufacturer, and for promotional purposes they had anchored this artificial island offshore that you could only get to by swimming. There was dance music on the island and a small bar. We would swim out there, climb up onto the island, and dance close together in our wet, clinging suits.

We all smelled of suntan lotion, in particular Nivea cream. Everybody used it. Because of all the dancing and kissing, the smell of Nivea still has a sexual connotation for me. It brings back a lot of fond memories of the Wannsee, which to me was always a very joyous place. Most people, however, remember the Wannsee for something else. It was at a villa on the Wannsee that Reinhardt Heydrich and Adolf Eichmann, and their aides came up with the Final Solution.

By now it was very clear to all of us kids that there was never going to be any return to normal life for Jews in Germany. My apprenticeship had, however, meant that my father had had to confront squarely the fact that neither of his children would inherit the button business.

Despite everything, I'm sure he had held on to this hope for a long time. To that extent, at least, Hitler did me (and my brother) a favor. If it weren't for the Nazis, my father would have insisted that I become a button merchant, and I wouldn't have been any better at it than Hans was. Sooner or later, I would have bolted, and I would have broken my father's heart. Instead, Hitler did that for me.

Yva was now in the same position my father had been in at the button factory. She was a creative power and had been for many years, but to officially fulfill the demand to "Aryanize," Yva's friend, the art historian Dr. Charlotte Weidler, took over the management of Studio Yva in name, in order that Yva could continue to run the studio. From then on she published her photographs under "Presse-Foto Yva." We youngsters, my friends and I, didn't think much about this; we just knew it was complicated. Despite all this, somehow we had a very, very good time until the very last days.

In 1935 or 1936, Yva received a very attractive offer from *Life* magazine to go to New York. Alfred, still believing that things would improve, talked her out of it. He didn't want to leave Berlin. He didn't speak English and couldn't see himself setting up a new life in New York.

I already knew that a photographer doesn't need language to be successful. When a photographer has a unique view of the world and its people, his or her work is highly paid and much sought after all over the world. Yva had that unique view, and that's why the offer came from America. She didn't follow it up because she listened to her husband.

I was aware of the danger of staying in the country. I was forever telling her that she should leave. She simply patted me on the head and said, "There, there, Helmut, nothing will happen to us."

After I left Berlin in 1938, Yva was sent to a concentration camp and was killed in Auschwitz. I have always done my utmost to keep her memory alive. She was a great photographer and an exciting woman.

IN THE LATE 1950s, June and I found ourselves in Berlin. Before our departure from Melbourne, I had given June a copy of Christopher Isherwood's book *Berlin Diary*. To me this book is the perfect introduction to the real "Old Berlin," and when we hit Berlin on our "Grand Tour" of Europe in that white Porsche, we lived, like Isherwood, in just such a pension, to our delight. Though June speaks no German, she immediately loved Berlin and the Berliners.

We arrived late at night to find that the hotels were all booked up for a convention. We queued in a hotel booking office in two different lines. June took the queue with a salesman at the head of it, and I took the queue with the salesgirl. June's turn came first. She waved an address in the air and said, "We're off!" She handed me the address in the taxi. We were headed for

Pension X at 45 Schluterstrasse, Yva's old studio. It was a very emotional taxi ride. By the time we reached our destination, I was all shook up.

The elderly couple behind the reception desk became suspicious and wary when I explained that before the war their pension had been a photographic studio that belonged to a famous photographer called Yva, and that I was once her assistant. I asked to be taken up to the fifth floor, where the studio used to be, but was told that I would have to wait until morning.

The following morning, we took the lift to the top floor to find the old studio intact—nothing had changed. The chandelier still hung from the ceiling, the boiserie was as good as new, the door handles too, and Yva's work still hung on the walls, but there was no sign of life. The proprietors breathed a sigh of relief when we finally left.

M Y   M O T H E R was very capricious, but around 1935–36 she became a tower of strength. The strength had left my father. I could see that. He was not capable of making any decisions, and she became the driving force behind the family's survival.

My father adored motorcars. His last car was a beautiful four-door Fiat. It had to be sold, because the Nuremberg racial laws forbade Jews to drive motorcars. The money was supposed to be put in the bank. Now, my father was the most law-abiding person in the world—there was not one law that he would have ever gone against. After the car was sold, my mother took the money away from him. She said, "You give me this money, I won't let you have it," because she knew my father was going to put it in the bank, and of course that would have been the end of that. The government would have confiscated it, as they did all Jewish bank accounts. She took the cash from the car sale and put it in the linen press, hiding it between the many sheets that were in the cupboard. Two years later, this money saved the family, because with it they were able to buy tickets for us to leave Germany.

THE END began on the 9th of November 1938, with the "Kristallnacht." The Nazis had a great talent for coining phrases: "The night of the long knives," Die Endlösung, Nacht und Nebel Aktion, and more.

During my apprenticeship with Yva, I also took a number of different courses on photography and filmmaking, somewhere downtown. One of these afternoons, I took the double-decker 19 bus.

I was sitting up on the top of the bus as we went down the Kurfürstendamm. When we passed Fasanenstrasse, I saw a big fire and heard a lot of noise. There was a big synagogue there.

I had no idea what had happened, but there was a lot of commotion and squads of storm troopers. The bus passed by and carried on down the Kurfürstendamm, where on the right-hand side there was a Jewish department store called F. B. Grunfeld, which was a beautiful building, built entirely of glass, in a very avant-grade architectural style.

It was being totally smashed by the storm troopers. As I progressed in the number 19 bus on my way to the lecture, I saw further evidence of the Kristallnacht.

When I arrived at the lecture, I received a telephone call from my mother. She said, "Helmut, don't come home. Your father has gone on a trip and they are looking for you." This was the code we all used when people were taken away to concentration camps. Of course after the lecture was finished I did have to go home. I wasn't carrying much more than bus fare. I wasn't prepared to go underground with no money, so I took the bus back to Friedrichsruherstrasse. My mother was distraught and very frightened. I took my little razor, whatever I needed, she gave me some money, and I left quickly.

Jewish men were being rounded up in the general sweeps all over Berlin. The Gestapo came to the door looking for me the next morning.

I went into underground hiding for two weeks. During the day, I was out on the streets. There was nowhere to hide; you could only hide in the evening. I had to be very circumspect. I would take care not to cross a street against a red light, because you always risked some traffic cop at the corner stopping you and asking you for papers you didn't have. If a Jew was caught going against a red light, he would invariably end up in a concentration camp. In the daytime I just tried to be as inconspicuous as possible, not to appear Jewish, just to be an everyday guy.

I often went to the movies, making sure to be on time for the newsreels— if you missed the newsreel and arrived late but in time for the film, you could be reported. All the newsreels included propaganda for Hitler. I would sit there with my heart beating fast as he ranted and raved against the Jews. I was never late.

The informers are still around in Germany and Austria. Recently, my assistant, finding nowhere to park the car near a restaurant in Berlin, parked it on the pavement. It was ten o'clock at night. An old guy comes by and pulls out a notepad and starts writing down our number. I said, "What the fuck are you doing?" He replied, "I'm going to report you." I said in Berlinese, "You fuck off, you old arsehole—go call the police!" I scared the shit out of him.

My first two or three nights in hiding were spent on the couch at Cousin Bennett and Elsa's apartment. As Bennett was an associate member of the SS, it was a pretty safe place for me to be, but Bennett was running a risk sheltering his Jewish cousin, and after two or three nights I moved on. I met other guys like me in the streets, and we exchanged information on where we could spend the night. I remember going out to Zehlendorf and staying in the big cellar of a villa that was owned by a Nazi Party member and was full of Jews. I wish I could remember his name, because the guy sheltered a great number, like fifteen Jews, in his cellar. The house of a party member was a pretty safe place to be.

Of course, going out to rich Uncle Edward's house was out of the question; he would have been too shit-scared to have me there, even though Uncle Edward thought nothing could touch him. He somehow forgot the fact that he was Jewish and was very happy with his Nazi cronies, who he thought would protect him forever.

Long after we had all left Germany, my parents and my brother too, I heard from my mother that poor Uncle Edward ended up in a concentration camp, because in one of the very rough Berlin winters during the war somebody told him he should shovel the snow from the front porch of his villa. He said, no way was he going to shovel, he was going to get somebody to shovel for him, this was no job for rich Uncle Edward. He was reported to a block warden and taken to a concentration camp, never to be heard of again.

We made the rounds, and I kept in touch with my mother, and after two weeks the heat was off. That meant they had rounded up all the Jews they could get. Being taken had nothing to do with being political; they were just Jews that had been rounded up in a general sweep and brought out to Oranienburg, which was a concentration camp quite near Berlin.

So once again my mother gathered up that energy that nobody had suspected she had. She had found out through some mysterious channels that there was a certain postbox at the Gestapo headquarters on Alexanderplatz where you could post a letter, a letter that would possibly obtain a release, or make it possible to leave the country. How she found that out, I don't know. She sat down and wrote a letter, and we went to Alexanderplatz and stuffed the letter into the postbox. Sometime not very much later, we received a summons to go to the Gestapo headquarters on Alexanderplatz.

We went up to the fifth floor. There was heavy security everywhere. We showed our papers to the guard and were directed to wait outside a particular office door. My name, "Helmut Neustaedter, the Jew," was called. My mother waited outside. In the office was a Gestapo officer. He was in mufti, not uniform.

I was ordered to stand in front of his desk. In the corner was another desk, staffed by a secretary with a typewriter.

No sooner did the door close than the Gestapo officer began abusing me at the top of his lungs, calling me a Jewish pig and shouting all kinds of insults that were à la mode in those days. He stopped his tirade to dispatch his secretary on an errand.

As soon as she had gone, his tone changed completely. He spoke very softly and very fast. He handed me the papers for the release of my father and told me exactly how and where to get myself a new passport. Until I had turned eighteen, just a couple of weeks before, I'd been too young to carry one of my own. He impressed on me the importance of getting a passport as soon as possible and of leaving the country immediately thereafter.

At that moment, the secretary returned to the room and the officer resumed his torrent of abuse. His parting words were, "Get out, you Jew bastard. Get out, you pig! GET OUT!" I left as quickly as I could, but I had got what I came for. I took my mother with me to the place where he had told me to apply for a passport, and they did indeed issue me one. It was valid for a year. On every page there was a big stamp, a bright-purple "J" for "Jew," but it enabled me to leave Germany. Once more in my life I was lucky. I had fallen on two good Germans.

With my passport secured, my mother bought me a railway ticket to Trieste and a second-class ticket on the *Conte Rosso*, a steamer bound for Tientsin, China.

She used the Fiat money from the linen press. I was due to leave on December 5. Less than a month had passed since Kristallnacht. The Nazis were hungry for foreign exchange, and currency controls were stringent. I was permitted to take the equivalent of just five dollars in cash with me, but I could take any goods and clothing I wanted. Although they were encouraging Jews to leave Germany, they made leaving expensive. Every departing Jew who left Germany had to pay an exit tax. After I packed my trunks and suitcases, I had to make a complete list of everything that was in them—every sock, every shirt, every suit. I took along as much as I could. I had a couple of cameras, including a Rolleicord and a Kodak, which I hoped would keep me in bread and butter for the next few years.

The officials checked the list and sealed my luggage. Then they worked out what they considered to be the new value of my stuff. That sum had to be paid in toto to the Nazi government. Once again, Mother's cache of Fiat money from the linen press came to the rescue.

Two days before I was due to leave, on December 3, my father came home. At least, the man who used to be my father came home. I was shocked when I saw him. He was frail and thin, but he was holding together. He had shrunk. They had made him smaller. He bore no evidence of bodily injury, he had not been physically harmed, but he had been wounded in every other possible way.

Running around naked day and night in temperatures below zero leaves no evidence of physical injury. He never told me what had happened to him. As soon as he returned, my mother booked a passage for the two of them to South America. Their boat was leaving in January. There was no question of them coming with me to China. There wasn't time for them to dispose of their household belongings before then, and in any event my father was in no condition to travel.

I treasured those last days with him, but I was heartbroken to see him that way. On the morning of December 5, 1938, I was ready to leave. All my trunks were at the door. My father sat me down and talked to me before we left the house. He looked like an old man. He told me he was very worried about me. He always called me "my dear boy" whenever he spoke to me. He loved me dearly, but he didn't have any illusions that his son, Helmut, was a serious person. I was what was called in German a "Windhund." He often called me that. He knew very well that all I wanted to do was to fuck girls, take photographs, and have a good time. I was just eighteen—it was the natural thing for a boy of my age to want to do.

After a final look at the house, my parents took me to the Bahnhof Zoo station and saw that my luggage was loaded on board the train. It was full of Jews traveling to Trieste for the same reason I was. I found my compartment and waved goodbye as we pulled out of the terminal.

I never saw my father again.

CHAPTER THREE
SINGAPORE, 1938–1940

BERLIN HAD FASCINATED ME from the moment I understood what a city meant. I loved it so much as a child. When I emigrated and left on my odyssey toward the Far East, I was very homesick for Berlin. I didn't give a shit about Germany or anything like that, but I was very, very homesick during those early days in Singapore, for the town, the ambience, for every little secret corner which I seemed to know.

I remember sitting by the port. I had no work, I lived on very little—scraps—and I used to see the ships come and go from Europe and I would cry my eyes out like a dog, because all I wanted to do was go back to Berlin. Even though I knew the Nazis were there and I knew perfectly well that it was an impossibility.

DURING THE LAST nights at home in Berlin, I lay in my bed, unable to go to sleep, with worries about how I was going to survive in Shanghai. Where was I going to sleep; was I going to end up in the gutter or starve to death? I was scared shitless.

Although China had struck me as exotic and intriguing, that had nothing to do with why it was my destination. I was going to China because there was quite simply no other place for me to go.

At this point very late in 1938, the American immigration quota and the English immigration quota were filled. Neither one was admitting any more German Jews into the country, unless you had £250 or £500, and who had that in those days? The only place still open, the only available safety valve, was China. There were no quotas. Most people went to Shanghai. All you had to do was get there.

Not that I was at all certain I wanted to get there. My mother, my friends, and I had all heard the stories which had filtered back to Berlin about the horrors of Shanghai. Rumors abounded, none of them good. It was said that there was no work and that many people had no place to sleep. We knew there had been fighting between the Chinese and the Japanese. It didn't sound like the ideal place for a young man to earn a living with a camera.

All I knew for certain about Shanghai was that my Tante Olga had lived there. Tante Olga had an irrational fear of being buried alive. She was afraid that one day she wouldn't wake up and that she would be put into a coffin and by the time she opened her eyes she'd be six feet under. Every night before she went to sleep she propped up a handwritten sign on her nightstand that read "Not Dead, Only Coma."

Tante Olga was from my mother's side of the family. She was a horse-woman and much admired by my mother because she was very adventurous.

She was married and widowed in Shanghai. After her husband died, she came back to Berlin. She used to tell us amazing stories about her life in China. She was crazy, but she was very amusing.

When my mother purchased my ticket on the *Conte Rosso* from the Lloyd Triestino Steamship Company, she had asked whether the ship was going on from Shanghai. She found out that for the same amount of money she could buy a ticket to Tientsin, which was farther north, not far from Peking. My now very practical mother realized that, by buying me a ticket to Tientsin, she was keeping my options open. If I didn't like the look of Shanghai, all I had to do was get back on the boat and keep going.

Of course, I had no idea whether Tientsin was likely to be any better than Shanghai. The terrible reports on the grapevine about Shanghai were recent, but we knew nothing whatsoever about Tientsin. It was a blank slate, a complete unknown, and the prospect of it terrified me.

I was petrified but, on the other hand, I was also quite elated. Despite my concern for my father, overall I was not sorry to be leaving. I'd been trying to get out of Germany since I was sixteen years old. Now it was happening. When I started thinking about what an adventure it was going to be, I just put China out of my mind. I loved the idea of traveling. Even more than that, I loved the idea of being away from home with nobody to tell me what to do.

We traveled through the night until we came to the Italian border. It was freezing bloody cold, because it was December. The German border guards were Gestapo or SS, and they came through the train. They knew perfectly well that it was full of Jews that were fleeing the country, and they were checking everybody's papers. Some of the passengers were hauled off the train in the middle of the night. It was my first time away from home, except for little trips to Denmark to visit my brother. I'd never been without my parents, I'd always had a very comfortable life; so, although it was the greatest adventure that ever happened to me, I was scared; I knew that if they hauled me off and put me in a concentration camp, that would be the end of me.

As it was, my "J"-for-"Jewish" passport was in order, and the train crossed into Italy and reached Trieste in the morning. The railroad depot was quite near the pier where the *Conte Rosso* was moored. This was no tramp steamer. I could see that it was a beautiful passenger liner. I saw my cabin trunks loaded onto the ship and boarded the *Conte Rosso* in great excitement. I had forgotten all my worries, all the nightmarish weeks before the departure when I would wake in the night shit-scared, wondering what was going to happen to me.

I went in search of my second-class cabin and was disappointed to find that I shared my quarters with three other men, all of whom were much older than I was.

I didn't much care for that, since I wasn't accustomed to a lack of privacy. The *Conte Rosso* left Trieste that evening, and as it passed Brindisi, the last European landfall, I stood at the stern of the ship and swore with all the fervor of an eighteen-year-old, "I will never, ever return to Europe."

After those few crocodile tears, I started to have a ball. I'd never had such a good time in my life. I could go out with women, and I could do whatever I wanted. I had quite nice clothes, because the clothes I had brought from Berlin were all rather chic. My father had given me some very good advice before leaving. He said, "My boy, even if you haven't got a penny in your pocket, when you leave your hovel, wherever you are living, you've got to look like a million dollars."

So a lot of the time I used to smuggle myself through the guarded door into first class. I had what was called "board money"—vouchers that could only be used on the ship. My mother had been able to use some of the money from the sale of the Fiat to buy me a tremendous supply of these vouchers, but hadn't dared to give me any more of it in cash than I was legally able to take out of the country. To be caught carrying extra hard currency was to risk being arrested as a Devisen Schmuggler, a very serious offense. If they found too much money on you, it was a surefire trip to the concentration camp. Every Jew leaving Berlin knew this. Nevertheless, some of the passengers who were removed from the train by the Gestapo at the Italian border were carrying concealed caches of money.

I met so many people on this ship—it was full of escaping, fleeing Jews. No one wanted to think about the terribly uncertain future. Everyone was having a wonderful time, drinking and carrying on. We were just having a ball. There was the strange atmosphere of dancing on a volcano; we all knew that once we got off the boat it was curtains.

Once off the ship, all I would have left would be the five dollars' worth of

Deutschemarks that I had in cash. But while I was on the boat, I had plenty of money to amuse myself, buy drinks, and have a good time—I was rich.

So I went to the dances in second class and I went to the dances in first class and I had a flirtation with a Viennese woman who was on board ship with her husband. She often came to visit me in my cabin when I had it to myself in the afternoons. Once I asked her, "How do you get away?" She answered, "Oh, I just tell my husband that I'm going to get my hair done." We used to fuck like mad. One day we were in bed in my cabin and hard at it and there was this tremendous bashing and thumping on the door. It was her husband, who was yelling, "I know you're in there. Come out at once!"

For a moment I thought my heart would stop. Astonishingly enough, the wife took no notice of it. When I realized he couldn't break the door down, I didn't let it bother me either. I just picked up where we had left off. It happened several more times thereafter. After the first time, I didn't pay attention to him and kept on screwing his wife.

I fucked my way across the Mediterranean and through the Suez Canal. I wasn't much interested in the young girls of my age. I sought out the older women, married ladies in their thirties. They had all the sex appeal, the glamour and the excitement that I was looking for. I was myself as a character in Stefan Zweig's "Burning Secret."

Suez was our first port of call. It was exotic but not somewhere I wanted to stay. The next stop was Djibouti. Djibouti was a hellhole, but an exciting docking nevertheless, since the Aga Khan and his beautiful young wife, the Begum Aga Khan, came on board. She had been a French showgirl before she married her husband.

A few years ago, she was seated next to me at a dinner party at Lynn Wyatt's house in the south of France and I said to her, "You know, you and I were on the same ship in 1938; you and your husband came aboard in Djibouti. It was 1938. You were so beautiful." She just looked at me. She hated my guts. She didn't want to know about me meeting her so long ago, she didn't want to hear about it, she didn't want to be reminded that she was as old as or older than I am.

At any of these ports, I'm sure we could have caught up on the news of the day. No one did. No one wanted to hear anything about life in the real world, away from the ship. I realized that this was my mother's last gift to me. By purchasing a ticket for the farthest possible destination, she was buying me a happy life for as long as she could. If the passengers could have stayed on the *Conte Rosso* forever, I think many would have chosen that lot in preference to going ashore.

One of the few male acquaintances I made on the ship was a man named Max Knopf, a gentle Prussian fellow with a big square head. A bookbinder by trade, he sort of looked after me. Herr Knopf told me that rumors were flying around the ship that it just might be possible to stay in Singapore. The rumor was that we would be reviewed by a committee that was looking for individuals with certain skills and crafts that were much in need in the city.

So, if one was lucky enough to be chosen by the committee, one would be absolutely saved, body and soul. I realized that because everybody was talking about it: Please, let's pray that we will be the ones chosen to land and live in Singapore.

Around Christmas Eve 1938, the *Conte Rosso* pulled into Singapore Harbor for a twelve-hour stopover. It was boiling hot, and the humidity was 99 percent; it felt like somebody had thrown a boiling-hot wet towel into your face. Everything was dripping. There was no wind. It was like that all year round. There are rainy periods, but the temperature always stays the same, and the humidity gets much worse when it rains.

The rumors were true: the Welfare Committee boarded the ship. Herr Knopf made sure I presented them with my credentials as a photographer. The committee stationed itself in the first-class dining room. They began screening the passengers who wanted to stay, which was everybody. Practically the entire ship queued up to be interviewed. They asked me my age, my profession, and my experience. One member of the committee was a petite, stylish woman with almost translucent white skin and dark-red fingernails. She seemed to have a sparkle in her eye as she looked me over and reviewed my résumé.

I was put aside as a possible candidate, and they called me back for a second interview. The fact that I was young, single, spoke English, and had my cameras with me was to my advantage. Finally, their decision was announced. I was selected. A member of the committee told me he could get me a position as a photographer with the *Straits Times*, the most important newspaper in Singapore. Herr Knopf was chosen to stay as well.

This was a great stroke of luck. Singapore was a part of the Straits Settlements. It was a British Crown colony, a little bit of England at the tip of the Malay Peninsula. Singapore was orderly. Singapore was clean. You could drink the water right out of the tap. To be granted permission to stay was to put an end to the speculation about the uncertainties of Shanghai. It was almost like being able to go to England itself. It was like winning the lottery.

I raced back to my cabin and quickly packed the steamer trunk, locked all my bags, and sent them ashore. It was Christmas Eve 1938, and admission into Singapore was the best Christmas present I had ever received.

My sense of economics told me that whether I had five dollars' worth of Deutschemarks or whether I didn't have five dollars' worth of Deutschemarks wasn't going to make any bloody difference. Somebody had told me on board ship that Chinese pussies were crosswise, so this was the moment to find out. Let's get rid of those five bucks. And so I went straight to a bordello and found out that was not the case.

The Welfare Committee put me into a sleazy boarding house in a seedy part of town and paid for my board and lodging. My room was a tiny wooden cell above the Chinese servants' quarters and garages, which must also have cost about five dollars a month. The low-class boarding house was run by an Australian couple. They were the first Australians I'd ever met. They were drunk twenty-four hours a day, screaming at each other and bashing each other up.

The sheets were changed when they were dark gray. There was a dirty gray mosquito net over the bed, but I needed it, filthy as it was, since the window could not be closed. Bamboo had grown into the room and grown out again, so the window was permanently jammed. Rats ran around in the rafters above, and a hairy-legged bird spider the size of my hand often dwelt beneath the sheets. There was a crisscross of wires under the ceiling so that the many flying foxes and large bats that flew into my window would be caught in the net. The book I was reading was *Dracula*. That frightened the shit out of me. It was terrifying.

During the Sino-Japanese War, there were still Japanese living in Singapore. Some of the Chinese would cut an ear off of a Chinese man if he was found trading with the Japanese, and one night I heard bloodcurdling screams coming from the Chinese quarters right below me. One of the Chinese houseboys had had his ears cut off by a compatriot right beneath my window.

I reported for work at the *Straits Times* and was put on the society beat. I was sent to tea parties at Government House. All the ladies wore tea gowns, and beautiful hats to protect them from the boiling sun. The men wore white cotton suits—always white. You had to have at least ten of them, because you perspired so much it was sometimes necessary to change twice a day during working hours. There might have been electric fans, but there was no air-conditioning, and in most cases the tepid, still air was moved by punkas pulled by native boys.

So there I was in my European double-breasted suit with a tie (I had no money to buy anything else), sweat dropping into the ground glass of my Rolleicord, trying to figure out the exposure, trying to set my camera, trying not to babble because I was so nervous. The ladies sort of looked at me and giggled; I got red in the face, I got flustered. By the time my camera was ready, the tea party was over. The event fizzled out and I came back with a little roll of film and developed it myself, sweating like a pig in the darkroom at the *Straits Times*.

The pictures were abominable—I mean unbelievable! I mean, there weren't any pictures! Let's face it, there was nothing! This situation repeated itself over and over. I never came up with anything the paper could use and often had no pictures at all. I lasted two weeks before I got the sack—out! I'd been sacked by the *Straits Times*. I was broke. Penniless!

Between the rats, the bugs, the Australians, and the Chinese, the boarding house seemed like a corner of bedlam, so I spent as little time there as I could. I didn't have any money to go to the movies, I went to the library. I read a great deal of Somerset Maugham, who had spent a lot of time in Singapore. I always liked reading about a place. It didn't matter if the story was exciting or not, as long as it was set in the place where I was living.

I also went to visit Max Knopf at his workshop. He was in somewhat better financial shape than I was. He was beginning to get customers. Since I had nothing else to do, I watched him work for hours on end. He had great big hands, and he used his thumb to make the gutters of the books. He always smelled of glue, and was very kind to me.

Max and I used to go out and eat together. We couldn't afford to go to European restaurants, or even the Chinese restaurants frequented by Europeans. We went to real Chinese dives, where we were the only Europeans in the joint. At first I was appalled by Chinese table manners. They shoveled the food into their mouths as fast as they could and made a great deal of noise doing it. But in all the restaurants we went to, the Chinese would all slurp away, and eventually Max and I started slurping away just like them. The food was great. You could eat yourself silly, and it cost about ten cents. Even so, sometimes he had to pay for me, because I had no money at all. We used to laugh a lot and talk about the good old days in Germany, and especially Berlin.

I was very fond of Herr Knopf; he was my only friend. I felt isolated and terribly homesick. I used to go down to Singapore's busy port and watch the bustling activity in the harbor. One of the more interesting events was the annual landing of a small convoy from England carrying single white women in search of husbands. There were many more European men than women in

Singapore. If a white English girl couldn't find a husband in Singapore, she was never going to find one. They called it "the fishing fleet."

On the wharf were the godowns where the ship coolies lived. The coolies or laborers who worked on the docks, like stevedores, unloaded the ships by forming a human chain, passing goods from hand to hand. It was brutal physical work. They slept in the godowns, vast open sheds on the wharf, which were made out of concrete with roofs but no windows, all packed together like sardines in the incredible heat. The kitchen was in there too. There were no bathrooms. I was shocked by the treatment of the Chinese and Malays by the colonials.

Despite my brave promise—that I had made on the deck of the *Conte Rosso* as we passed Brindisi—of never returning to Europe, I wanted to go "home." Given all the Japanese activity in China, I knew that I was better off in Singapore than in Shanghai or Tientsin, but I certainly wasn't "home." I was even more miserable when I considered that the "home" I used to know really didn't exist anymore.

I kept all this from my parents, of course. I wrote them letters, but I didn't want to worry them. They had enough problems of their own. They left Germany for South America early in 1939, but they had to leave almost everything behind. I couldn't bring myself to tell them that I didn't have any money. That, I wasn't going to do.

After one of my days spent watching the harbor, I returned to the boarding house to find a note waiting for me. It was from Madame Josette Fabien, the woman who had been on the Welfare Committee on the *Conte Rosso*. She was inviting me to lunch.

Josette Fabien was thirty-four years old, a small woman with long red fingernails, blond hair, a sharp nose, a wide sensual mouth, blue eyes, and white transparent skin. She wore clinging dresses and wide full pants. Because of the heat, the dresses were very thin. She never wore stockings.

She ran a successful business printing and selling advertising in theater programs and menus for hotels and restaurants. Her office was in the Raffles

Hotel. After that first lunch, she took me on several afternoon outings. I was flattered to become the friend or occasional companion of such a glamorous, sophisticated creature who spoke French, Malay, and English fluently.

There had been a strong sexual attraction to this older woman who lived in a suite in the Raffles Hotel. She seemed to take a motherly interest in me. Eventually, I was invited for dinner in the Palm Court, which was the grand ballroom of the Raffles Hotel.

The ballroom was long and wide with open arches that gave out on the street. There were beautiful palm trees and God knows what else in there. There were huge electric ceiling fans—everything was electric. Even the beautiful little lights on the tables were electric. It had a big dance floor, and at the end of the room it had a stage with a big dance orchestra. At midnight the orchestra leader struck up the signature tune, "Music Maestro Please," to signal the end of the dinner.

Then I would be asked up to her suite, which had large rooms filled with big dark furniture. A terrace gave out onto the interior courtyard of the hotel. As the friendship progressed, I seem to remember that we'd leave the ballroom earlier and earlier, until I could hear the signature tune wafting up to her apartment from the ballroom below, while I was holding Josette in my arms and kissing her.

Then she would break away; it was a teasing kind of relationship. I tried to seduce her, but I didn't know how to go about it, so we started with kisses and it became more passionate but it always broke up. She'd say that she was the equivalent of a cradle snatcher and tell me that I could be her son, and, of course, I'd get very excited about all that. It took quite a while before Josette decided that she might as well sleep with me because the thing had already gone so far, so one night she succumbed and we went to bed together, in her big bed with the big stark white mosquito net floating around us, and became lovers.

One night, to escape the heat of the room, she was standing on the terrace looking out over the city. She had nothing on. I came up behind her and took her from the back.

I never stayed the night at the hotel. I used to take a rickshaw back to the boarding house, since it was too far to walk. Most of the coolies who pulled rickshaws were opium smokers. Until they got a fare, they sat with their opium pipes, puffing away. At that time in Singapore, opium was a legal but controlled substance. If you were an addict, you had to register with the government. Once you were registered, you got your regular weekly ration at special government opium stores.

I was fascinated by the rickshaws. At first it was terrifying to see the coolies pulling them for the local people. The colonials were used to it, but as I said the way they treated the Chinese and the Malays was unbelievable. They were worse than slaves.

The rickshaw drivers wore loincloths and big coolie hats. They were barefoot, and I remember the sound of their naked feet slapping the pavement as they ran through the quiet city. You could see their ribs, could hear them breathe—they went pretty fast, but you could hear this terrible breathing from the effort of pulling. I was usually the only passenger, but sometimes there'd be three people in a rickshaw. When they went uphill in the steamy heat, the breathing got slower and slower and heavier and heavier. I became a regular late-night rickshaw passenger, as evening found me in Josette's bed three or four nights a week.

Josette's bed at the Raffles, like all beds in Singapore, had a bolster called a Dutch wife. A Dutch wife was a skinny pillow that you put between your legs so that you didn't get prickly heat. The rash was very unpleasant, and the only way to get rid of it was to wash with Lifebuoy soap, a soap that was almost as bad as the rash itself. Even small children slept with a Dutch wife between their legs, so there was no rubbing between body parts.

When Josette and I made love the first time, I placed the Dutch wife under her ass to raise up her hips. As soon as I did this, she covered her face with her hands. She had beautifully manicured hands, with a ring and a gold bracelet that she never took off. I tried to drag her hands away from her face, but she fought me, saying, "No! I don't want you to see my face. I don't want you to see my eyes while we're making love."

From then on, whenever we were fucking, she always kept her hands in front of her face.

She lived very well, but in Singapore in those days that was not so difficult. Singapore was a free port, and many of life's luxuries, including liquor, cigarettes, jewelry, and automobiles, came in duty-free and were quite inexpensive. Josette had an American car, a huge black Chevrolet. She also had a chauffeur, a native Malay. Most Europeans did.

I remember one outing to the country to see a friend of hers, an English engineer who was building bridges and roads for the government. He had been her lover many years before. We took the car and the driver. I wore a pair of linen shorts, a white shirt, and white knee socks.

On the way back into town, Josette unzipped my fly and began giving me a blow job as we were driving along. It was twilight, and night was coming on fast, but even so, it must have been obvious to the Malay chauffeur what was going on: there was no partition between the back and front seats. I was astonished—no one had ever given me a blow job before—and certainly not with an audience. When we got back to the hotel, the crotch of my linen shorts was all smeared with dark-red lipstick.

I don't believe Josette was concerned about the driver seeing us at all. To Josette and to many other Europeans in Singapore, the Malays and the Chinese were nonpersons, lesser beings. What they did and what they saw was of no importance.

I went back to Singapore with June in 1956. We went to the Kodak offices, because I needed some film. We were asked to sit down and wait for the manager. He was very nice, but when he called in an elderly male assistant, he called him "boy." They always called them "boy," but June was outraged by the way he addressed this person. A kid straight from school in England, who'd never been in an office, got three or four times the salary of the Chinese that ran the office. The Chinese were clever, orderly, and highly intelligent. They ran the offices but they got nothing; they were considered the lowest form of humanity, even in 1956. June was horrified.

In Singapore as in Berlin, prostitution was big business and was conducted openly. Ever since my brother had pointed out Red Erna, I'd been fascinated by the idea that you could buy love. I loved bordellos. All my sexual experiences had been with girls from good bourgeois families. The women on the ship had been from the same social strata; they were just a little older.

There was a place called Chaney Alley where the pimps waited for customers right alongside the rickshaw coolies. They used to stand on the street—which was not very well lit—and smack their fingers and thumbs together, saying, "You can fuck my sister—virgin, virgin—come fuck my sister!" They would duck down a lane and drag out the young Chinese girls by their thin pigtails and hold them up and say, "Which one you want? Which one you want to fuck? Guaranteed virgin!" And then, if you said "No thank you," they'd chuck the girls back down the dark lane.

Infidelity was commonplace. There were even rules governing love affairs, however. The English have a crude saying: "The niggers begin in Calais." No one gave a damn if you were fucking another English gentleman's wife, as long as you were discreet about it, but having an affair with someone who was not British was frowned upon, and an affair with a non-European was strictly taboo. For a British colonial, the worst thing you could do was to have an affair with a native.

The men did it anyway. The young Europeans who started working at the age of twenty-three or so in the banks and import-export companies commonly took Chinese, Malay, or Eurasian mistresses. These women were never seen in public. Often they lived upcountry, outside the city. Frequently they bore children by their lovers.

Every European who had worked in Singapore for four years got six months of what was called "home leave" to go back to England or Holland or wherever he came from. It was just long enough to pick out a European bride. When the young man returned to Singapore, his new wife came with him. Sometimes he kept both his mistress and his wife; sometimes he didn't. Either way, the mistress was in a much-diminished position.

Because this pattern repeated itself over and over, mistresses knew that home leave was a time of danger. A mistress who suspected that her man was going home to select a wife was likely to consult a witch doctor for some preventive black magic. She would take him an object belonging to her lover; often it was a silver cigarette case. The witch doctor would put a spell on the lover through the object, after which the mistress would return it to her man, packing it in his luggage for his journey home.

Many Europeans feared the power of witchcraft. Rumors abounded of Englishmen who took sick and died on the voyage home, but the accounts were like reports of the Indian rope trick. Everybody had heard about these instances, on very good authority, but no one had actually witnessed one. In Australia, the Aborigines obtain amazing results by "pointing the bone" at a victim. Even if he is several miles away, it has often been known to work. Again, the victim usually dies of a mysterious illness.

Josette put her business sense to work on my behalf and decided that I might be able to make a living as a portrait photographer. Through her advertising-and-printing business, she knew the manager of Robinson's Department Store on Raffles Square and got me set up in a space on the top floor. In the back of the space I made a little photo studio with two lamps, my tripod, my Rolleicord, and some fabric that I got from the store to use as a backdrop. Robinson's let me use furniture or anything else I needed as props and agreed to advertise for me for free until I built up a clientele. A beaded curtain separated the studio from the front office, or reception room. Out in front of the studio were two easels with samples of my work on them, taken from Josette's theater programs.

I called myself Marquis. Josette had little books made up. They had gold covers with my name and the studio name engraved on the front. The idea was to glue the proofs from the photo sessions into the books to present to the clients, but unfortunately I didn't have many clients. I don't think I even had one customer a day. I just sat there behind a Chinese table, totally bored and surrounded by Chinese furniture, waiting for customers who never turned up.

One day the Sultan of Jahore arrived with his three kids, two young princes and a princess. They asked me to come to the Palace of Jahore and teach the boys about photography, and I thought that was great.

I started being seen around Singapore with Josette and her family, including her younger sister Kitty. On Sundays, Josette would take me, Kitty, Kitty's husband, Dick, and their two daughters to the Seaview Hotel for what in colonial language was called "Sunday tiffin," an elaborate lunch consisting of many courses and taking hours to serve. All of European Singapore went there to see and be seen. It was the place to go. Buckets of pink gins and Tiger Beer were consumed, and then, when the kid Helmut had done his duty and promenaded Kitty's children, it was home to bed to fuck all afternoon. It was, after all, what everyone did after Sunday curry tiffin.

Kitty and Josette had a strange relationship. Eight years previously, when Josette was still living in Java, her husband had gone on a trip to Europe. Kitty, who was a couple of years younger than Josette and more attractive, was in Europe at the same time. The two found themselves in the same city, and then in the same bed. They had a wild affair. Josette might never have known a thing about it, except that Kitty told her everything as soon as she got home. There ensued a terrible drama between the two sisters, and when the husband returned, Josette confronted him with his infidelity and filed for divorce. After the split, however, the two sisters patched it up.

Kitty lived a sexually adventurous life. Her husband, Dick, was a sea captain on the KPM steamer that ran between Java and Singapore. He was away all week and came home only on weekends. While he was gone, Kitty entertained her lover, a Hungarian violinist who played with the dance orchestra in the Palm Court of the Raffles Hotel. When Dick left at dawn on Monday, the fiddler moved in for the week. Saturday morning found Kitty with binoculars, standing on the balcony of her apartment, scanning the horizon for

Dick's ship. As soon as she saw it pull into Singapore Harbor, she sent her lover packing: "Out you go and I'll see you on Monday." Like a good Belgian wife, Kitty was very economical. She served the fiddler's warmed-up leftover Friday-night dinner to her husband on Saturday. Likewise, the violinist got the husband's warmed-up Sunday leftovers for Monday supper.

Once a week Kitty volunteered at the Seamen's Mission, which was a bit like the USO canteen. Whenever freighters came into port, sailors of various European nationalities would be turned loose in Singapore with a bit of money and nowhere to go. Most of them were French, Dutch, or English. At the Seamen's Mission, they could get a free meal, a little entertainment, and a hot shower. It was fashionable for society ladies to go to the Seamen's Mission and serve tea to the sailors, noblesse oblige and all that.

Kitty, however, often had an ulterior motive for going there. She used to pick up young sailors and take them home to her house after the mission closed at 10 p.m., while her husband was at sea and her violinist lover was fiddling away at the Raffles. She used to give them liquor and then wheel them out on one of those chaises longues that had wheels in front. You could lift it up and wheel it around, and she'd wheel them straight out of the living room into the garden and lay them under the stars.

How Kitty managed this three-ring sexual circus with her two daughters around is beyond me. She never told me any of this, of course, but Josette made sure I knew all about it. Josette was an extremely jealous woman, and she was aware of her sister's beauty and her insatiable sexual appetite. Josette warned me early on that if she ever caught me in bed with Kitty she'd slit my throat from ear to ear. From her tone of voice, there was little doubt that she meant every word of her threat. This is the same woman who used to complain that she couldn't hit the chauffeur or beat her servants anymore because she said they would go to the police and complain about her. She just couldn't understand why she was no longer allowed to do this.

Now, Singapore was a place where if you coughed or farted everybody would know about it within five or six hours. It was the most closely knit society. There were only about eight thousand Europeans living there—most of them English—and half a million Chinese. The white locals were very disapproving of the fact that Josette was having an affair with this young man who, as they saw it, was nothing but a gigolo. They were right—I had become a gigolo. I knew what a gigolo was, because I'd seen gigolos as a kid in the hotels. I don't know how I felt— I don't know if I was amused or ashamed—I can't remember. But I do know that I was totally fitted out in the most beautiful suits and beautiful shirts that didn't cost much money, all made to order by a Chinese tailor and paid for by Josette. I looked like a million bucks.

The whole of Singapore knew exactly what was going on, and within a very short time we became a scandal, to the extent that I was called into the office of the director of Robinson's Department Store, who said it had come to his attention that I was carrying on this liaison and that it was very bad for me.

Josette too was told that she should break up with me. She, of course, had a great deal more to lose than I did. Her whole professional life and livelihood was at stake. If her clients boycotted her because of her affair with me, her thriving business would turn sour pretty quickly. As a divorcee, her social position was already a bit tenuous. Despite Kitty's far more outrageous behavior, her social standing was much higher than Josette's, because she was a "proper" married woman. In any event, Kitty was a great deal more circumspect about her love affairs than Josette and I were.

In fact, local society not only frowned upon our relationship but also told us quite bluntly that unless we stopped our affair we would both be ostracized. By that time, however, our sexual relationship had advanced by leaps and bounds. I could do it day and night, like every kid of eighteen or nineteen. I mean, I was the perfect age. I was already reasonably sexually proficient when I got to Singapore, and what I didn't know, I learned very quickly. Josette was a woman of great experience. There was very little that she couldn't teach me.

Despite the threats, Josette was unwilling to terminate our affair. I was too good in bed. Our sex wasn't joyous, it was steamy—"schwül," in Schnitzler's terminology. Love in the emotional sense had nothing to do with it. We were addicted to fucking. Josette blamed it on the climate. She used to tell me that the heat and humidity, rather than making you tired, made you want to fuck a lot. She opted to keep me.

She made one change: she moved out of the Raffles and took a big house in Changi, where the prisoner-of-war camp was during the war. It was right on the beach—in front of the house was the China Sea. There were just the two of us, plus the cook and the maid and the chauffeur.

I transferred all my belongings in my steamer trunks into the house. The trunks were filled with clothing Josette had bought for me. I no longer had a place to live that was separate from hers. Shortly after we moved in, we celebrated my nineteenth birthday. She presented me with a watch. It was sterling silver, with a watchband made of heavy chain link. She had it inscribed, "To Bébé from Josette." With the gift of that watch, my transition was complete. I was a true gigolo.

I loved that house in Changi. I was very happy there. There was a sukiyaki house next door which we went to sometimes for dinner because it was within walking distance. Geishas use to come—not for sex, just for entertainment. They cost very little money, and they came with a portable gramophone, put it down on the floor, wound it up, then danced to the record. It was entertainment—a classical dance.

I was able to swim again. I hadn't been able to train since I'd arrived, almost a year earlier. I had tried to on one of our outings upcountry. I had dived into the river, which was really stupid of me. I never got out of the water so fast—there were big water snakes swimming next to me. They were all poisonous. The river was also full of crocodiles. In Singapore, snakes and crocodiles were a hazard of daily life. In town, the storm drains were very deep. They had to be, to handle the tropical downpours.

Quite frequently after one of these torrential rains, crocodiles and cobras would be flushed out of the storm drains and onto the city streets, even in the middle of the business district.

Upcountry it was worse. Josette and I often went to a very chic nightclub just outside the city, called Coconut Grove. To get there you had to drive through a park, which was quite overgrown but very beautiful. Everyone knew not to get out of the car and walk through the park. Nobody in his right mind would have done that. To stroll through the park was an invitation to be killed by a king cobra.

In Changi I swam every day in the China Sea. I had to do my kilometer in the morning, because by the afternoon the water was too hot to go swimming. I also had a little sailboat. One day I was caught way offshore with it when the tide was going out. It was just before noon, and the sun was scorching. The heat was incredible. The boat had a rope attached to the bow. I had to jump into the water and tow the boat through the mud of the receding tide back to shore. It took me a couple of hours to slog my way back to the beach. My shoulders and back were on fire. Sleeping was very painful, and I blistered and peeled for weeks.

No European in the Far East ever slept naked, despite the heat. You sweated a lot at night, and if a breeze came in through the window, you'd get a chill, followed by a cold in your tummy and a helluva case of diarrhea. The stomach, therefore, always had to be covered in bed. What you wore to bed was very important, however. The British believed that, the moment you started wearing a sarong, that was the beginning of the end.

When I landed in Singapore, the first thing I was warned about was never to go native. Even Josette's former lover, the engineer, always wore a dinner jacket to his evening meal—even upcountry, even when he was dining all by himself. It was part of the colonial discipline. At times it was hypocritical, and in many ways it was ridiculous, but it served the British very well and made them ever mindful of the fact that they were the masters.

Since leaving Berlin I'd been wearing pajamas, but with my Changi sunburn they were much too painful. The sarong is a very simple, beautiful garment that is ideally suited to protecting the stomach from drafts. It didn't hurt my shoulders, so I abandoned my PJs and started wearing a sarong. Once my sunburn healed, I never put my pajamas on again. To the English, that simple act would have signified the beginning of my decline and fall. Yeah, you are not one of us anymore. I wasn't one of the colonial masters anymore. I had put down my White Man's Burden and defected to the other side.

We didn't hear much about the war in Europe in Changi, but after the fall of Poland there wasn't much to tell. Skirmishes at sea continued, but it was winter on the continent and nothing much was happening on land. The *Straits Times*, among others, took to calling it the "phony war." However, from my trips down to the harbor I knew that ships like the *Conte Rosso* carrying Jewish refugees had stopped coming to Singapore. It was apparent that it had become all but impossible to leave Germany.

After about six months in Changi, Josette decided we had to move back into town. It was spring 1940. I suspect she wanted to move because it was difficult for her to run her business from so far out in the country. She rented a flat on the fourth floor of the Capitol Building, an elegant apartment house on the corner of Orchard Road. We still had a cook, maid, and chauffeur. Even though we lived on the fourth floor, there were no apartments beneath us. Everything below was taken up the by the Capitol Cinema, one of the most prominent movie houses in Singapore. Although I was reluctant to give up my daily swim in the China Sea, I was delighted to be so close to the movies again. We both loved them.

I was also glad to be back in town for another reason. During our stay in Changi, I had had little contact with anyone but Josette. I'd been screwing her daily for the better part of a year. I was obliged to perform sexually more than I cared to. The passion had begun to flag.

She set me up with my own room in the apartment. It had just a single bed, since all the serious fucking took place in her bedroom. She used to come and sit on the side of my bed and try to coax me into coming into her room, but I didn't want to do it anymore. I was bored. I invented headaches, stomach aches—anything to avoid having to screw her.

To alleviate the boredom of my liaison with Josette, I found excuses to go out at night. There were a number of amusement parks in Singapore, including three called the "New World," the "Happy World," and the "Old World"— big amusement parks with Chinese theaters, outdoor theaters, restaurants, a kind of Luna Park, and stands where you could buy Chinese and Malay food. The center of attraction was what was called the cabaret—a big round building. As you came in, you bought dance tickets, because there were taxi dancers, or hostesses, available on a big round dance floor. Around the dance floor were tables on the same level, and then there was another level with more tables, slightly raised.

The taxi dancers sat on the first level—down on the level of the dance floor. The customers could come alone or with their girlfriends or wives, and sat on the raised podium that ran around the dance floor. The lavatories were next to each other: "Gentlemen," "Ladies," and then, next to the "Ladies," "Hostesses." An interesting separation I had never experienced in Europe.

The girls were extremely attractive. The Chinese are very good dancers. I had a little pocket money. Maybe I got it from Josette—I don't think I made very much money in my photographic studio in Robinson's Department Store. It was enough to go out and have a simple meal; Chinese meals cost next to nothing in Singapore in those days.

I danced a lot with a taxi dancer called Anita Gonzales. I rather fancied her and she me. We danced together quite often, and one time she put her legs between mine and brought me on, until I had an orgasm right there on the dance floor. We palled up, and she invited me to her house—a tiny little bungalow on a dusty road in a dubious part of Singapore away from the main part of the city.

Like the other taxi dancers, Anita Gonzales was not a professional whore but she did receive clients outside of working hours. I made a date, and she told me she'd leave a light on in a certain part of the house when she was free. So, hot and bothered, I arrived at the house as soon as I could. I saw that a light was on, but it was in another room, which meant that she had a client, a friend, whatever with her. So I drove around the block about ten times, getting more and more impatient. After perhaps an hour, the signal was given and I went into Anita's house. We didn't muck about much, we got down to fucking very quickly.

Something very funny happened just before I fucked her. Anita was Filipino and had a lot of crucifixes and holy pictures hanging in the bedroom. She very carefully covered all the holy pictures with little white handkerchiefs, because she didn't want to be making love to somebody with all those holy people looking on.

I was less successful with the most famous dancer of the Old World, who called herself the Bengal Tiger. She was very beautiful and well known all over Singapore. She was a White Russian who had come to Singapore via Shanghai. She had flaming-red hair and very pale skin. I tried very hard to screw the Bengal Tiger, but I had no luck.

One night I came home around two o'clock in the morning. Josette was waiting up for me. She knew I'd been out with a girl and she was furious. I tried to lie my way out of it, but my excuses were pretty lame. I knew I couldn't very well tell her that I'd been with Herr Knopf.

It was an ugly scene. She was so angry that she began pounding me on the chest with her fists. I finally had to get a coat hanger to fend off the blows. She kept pummeling me and screaming, "I'm keeping you, I'm buying you. I give you pocket money, I make it possible for you to dress yourself—and you, you little bastard, you go out with these whores!"

After that, getting away from Josette became more important than ever. I spent a lot of time holed up at the library, just like I had when I first arrived.

I gravitated from books to magazines and began coming across marvelous photographs by people like Brassai and George Hurrell. Suddenly my desire to become a photographer came flooding back to me. I started thinking about Yva and how ecstatic I'd been working in her studio. While in Singapore, I'd lost all professional ambition. I'd become totally lethargic about my career. I realized how far I was from the goal I'd set for myself of becoming a *Vogue* photographer. Instead I'd become a trained fucker.

I became fed up with the whole thing. I wanted to be on my own. I had a great desire to be with young people. I was nineteen, and all of a sudden I realized that I was spending all of my time with a woman who was almost double my age. The only time I was with young people was when I took Kitty's two little girls around the amusement park on Sundays. Sometimes Kitty, her husband, Josette, and her friends wanted to be alone too, to talk about things that they didn't want me to hear. I was a kid to them.

Josette's attacks of jealousy continued, and I still went out and didn't come home until three in the morning. So it was becoming very dicey indeed between us. I realized that I had to get away, that it would be the end of me if I stayed. Morally, in every possible way—if I spent more years of my life in Singapore, I would be finished.

I still worked in my studio and managed to get a few portrait commissions. One of them was from a very beautiful Eurasian woman who was married to a Chinese dentist. They were quite wealthy but totally ostracized. The Chinese husband was ostracized by the Chinese community, and the Eurasian wife was never received in either Chinese or European society. When the prints from her sitting were ready, I brought them to her house one afternoon when she was alone. She was very satisfied with my work; she did not pay me but offered to go to bed with me there and then, and for good measure threw in her two-seater Chrysler, with a dickey seat and an enormously big wooden steering wheel. I had always, from early boyhood, been crazy about motorcars and accepted both offers enthusiastically.

The affair was always consummated in her house, which was decorated in a strange mixture of European decor, European furniture (or, rather, what the Singaporeans thought was elegant European furniture, which had nothing to do with what was elegant in Europe), and fairly cheap Chinese bric-a-brac and Chinese furniture.

Singapore was always referred to as a first class place for second-class people.

CHAPTER FOUR

AUSTRALIA, 1940–1942

A S   T I M E   P A S S E D, the threat of local war became much greater. I remember an evening at the Capitol Cinema with Josette when they interrupted the screening of *Gone With the Wind* to announce that the Nazis has overrun Belgium and entered France.

Nobody knew what to make of it, because we were so far removed from the scene of European war; people thought nothing could touch them, guarded as they were by the British fleet and the British army in this stronghold of Singapore. Yet, as time went on, it was obvious that Singapore was going to fall. The Japanese were making their way through Siam—moving through the jungle toward Malaya.

We became aware of two terrible military disasters for the British. The sinking of two of the most important battleships—the *Repulse* and the *Prince of Wales*. These two enormous, powerful British battleships were sunk by the Japanese just outside Singapore Harbor. There was some censorship, in that the government of the Straits Settlements did not tolerate any criticism of military defenses as planned by the authorities.

For instance, big naval guns pointing out to sea were cemented into the rocks of Singapore—the hills surrounding the port—so that their direction could not be changed. Nobody ever considered the possibility of the Japanese attacking through Siam—coming the back way through the jungle and attacking from behind the guns.

A number of British and American journalists were thrown out of Singapore because they had written articles criticizing the conservatism of the local defenses, of the army and the navy and the local authorities. Also, the country had a history of arbitrary deportation, which meant that the Straits Settlements government could ask anybody of any nationality to leave the colony within forty eight hours without giving any reason.

If the person was destitute and European, the government would pay for a steerage ticket to Europe. I knew some journalists who were asked to leave just before the Japanese invasion because they had criticized the local authorities. But the deportations dated back all the way to Somerset Maugham's days; he probably wrote the most revealing stories.

I had already escaped certain death at the hands of the Nazis. I had developed quite a nose for when to get out of a place—I had a strong sense of self-preservation. My German passport, stamped "J" for "Jew" on every page, was due to expire twelve months after my departure from Berlin, and the only way to renew it was to go to the German Consulate in Singapore.

I was not about to walk into the lions' den, so I just let my passport lapse. That made me a stateless citizen without any papers, totally at the mercy of any authority. I was a man without a country.

Of course, I did have a pretty good idea that I could have problems getting away from Singapore and entering into another country. At a young age I had read *Beau Geste* and found something very romantic about the East and the Foreign Legion. I toyed very seriously with the idea of joining the Legion in Singapore, where there was a recruiting center. I reasoned that if I really had to leave Singapore I'd join up, because it was one way of getting a nationality; when you got out they gave you a French passport.

In the end, however, my good Jewish sense prevailed. I told myself it would be a bit drastic, and God knows what would happen to me. Whatever it was, it was going to hurt and it was not going to be very amusing. It was going to be a shooting thing, and very rough physically. I was a fucker, not a fighter. I gave up the idea.

But now, German Jews were regarded as a fifth column. There was talk about internment. They used to say: Maybe you should intern all these people? But where would they go? Maybe we should send them away? But it was loose talk, it was conjecture, more or less. Terrible things can take a long time to happen. There's a sort of slow evolution. The evolution can last a week, it can last a month. Anyway, they decided we weren't going to escape—where would we go to? I mean, we weren't going to go into the jungle—not a whole lot of Berlin Jews! Give me a break, that was not in the book!

The fact that I was a stateless person had not made much difference while I was in Singapore, while there was no war, but once war had broken out in Europe, I became an enemy alien. Although I was stateless, they knew where I came from. I was an enemy alien on English territory. We all were—there must have been about two hundred of us that had come off the *Conte Rosso*.

Nothing dramatic happened. As I said, everything always happens very slowly. You get lulled into a kind of lethargy, a false sense of security. When it starts, it's very late in the cycle. You don't usually suffer physical pain. If something drastic like that were to happen, you'd make your getaway. Instead, it happens slowly—you get used to it—and another law gets passed.

The same thing happened in Germany in 1933 and 1934, when they said: "The owner of this button factory is a Jew. All right, as of the first of March, he can still work here but the boss will be Mr. So-and-so, who is an Aryan and who has been in the company for a long time. He will look after the money, and he will need some money." It was a slow process, a legal process, which is much more dangerous than anything that happens suddenly.

One day I got a notice from the police saying, "You will be interned on such-and-such a date"—in about a month. "The assembly point is at Wharf

10. You are allowed to take all your personal belongings but you are not allowed to take your motorcar. You have to sell your motorcar."

And everybody turns up on the set date at a certain hour at the assembly point. It is as simple as that. Kafkaesque.

I just said, "Jesus Christ, just my luck!" I now had a perfect excuse to get away from Josette. I was going to move on to some other place—no one knew where, because they didn't tell us where they were going to ship us. All I knew was that I was going to get out and that all my friends were going to come with me, the guys I knew from Berlin or Germany. We were all going to be together.

What's more, I was not going to be in a fucking war, I was not going to see any fucking Japanese, I was not going to see Josette anymore!

For the second time I was leaving—I was in seventh heaven. I got rid of my motorcar—I gave it back to the lady who had given it to me—and went off to the rendezvous point. What do I see there? What lies in the port? In the port lies the *Queen Mary*, which had been fitted out as a troopship.

I climbed on board with my trunks and my little camera and moved into a very nice cabin with a couple of other guys. So began another chapter in my life.

We had no idea where we were going. We thought India. Nobody ever thought of Australia. I mean, whoever thought of Australia? Nobody thought of Australia. You didn't go to Australia! Leaving had solved two problems for me—Josette and the prospect of war in Singapore—and I wasn't very much concerned where I would end up.

WE LIVED IN absolute luxury on the *Queen Mary*. We were under guard but not very strictly, because obviously we weren't going to jump overboard. There were British troops on the ship already. We were treated beautifully. We had printed menus with the ship on them, just like proper passengers.

The air-conditioning was not very efficient. It was boiling hot in the cabin and in the public rooms, and one night, about three or four days out of Singapore, the porthole of the cabin was open to get some fresh air. I woke up at about three o'clock in the morning and felt a cold blast of air come into the cabin through the porthole. That is when I realized what my destination would be.

By working out how much time had lapsed since our departure from Singapore, I became sure that the destination of the *Queen Mary* was going to be Australia.

When we arrived at Port Melbourne, we were transferred onto trains whose windows were nailed shut. Our first stop was Seymour Station, where I first tasted an Aussie culinary delight—a meat pie—the publicity for which read, "Four and twenty in everybody's mouth," under a picture of a flock of blackbirds flying out of a pie. Most off-putting. I didn't want a pie that had been in everybody's mouth.

Our final destination was Tatura One Internment Camp, not far from Melbourne. Each of these internment camps consisted of four compounds— A, B, C, and D—with observation towers and barbed-wire fencing. In one of the compounds there were only single women, in one there were men, in one married couples, and I can't remember what was in the fourth. Tatura Two housed what were referred to as enemy aliens, who were all Aryan Germans of Nazi convictions.

In the internment camp I was in with my mates, we were all Jews or communists and termed anti-Nazi. There were a lot of bush telegraphs going back and forth between the two camps, the Nazi camp and the anti-Nazi camp. Most of the news was distorted and came through our guards, elderly Australian soldiers who had been called up. Their education was elementary, to say the least, but they were kindness personified to all of us.

The food was good and plentiful, and in our compound we had some professional cooks who did wonders with the army rations we were given. We were sleeping two to a room in barracks of twenty-four very simple rooms.

They were long corrugated-iron huts, terribly cold in the winter and boiling hot in the summer. Above the window there was a kind of open chicken-wire ventilation system, and in the summer tremendous dust storms of red sand blew up. Even though we shut the window, the chicken-wire ventilation let through gusts of red sand that covered everything that was in our huts, inches deep. The food too—the soups, the porridge—everything was full of red sand. A Berlin boy like me had never experienced anything like it.

A hierarchy was established in the camp, a state within the state. A government and a representative were chosen with full support from the Australian commandant at Tatura. Each compound held 250 people. Each camp held a thousand. There was a regular weekly assembly with a president and a Parliament where people would argue endlessly about the running of the camp.

I shared my room with a guy called Wally Würzburger, who was a very gifted musician and possessed a fabulous sense of humor. We decided to set up house together. We were very happy. We used to sit outside our front door, on the steps. Of course, there was no back door. Wally composed music. He used to compose it in his head while he was doing camp jobs. We all did camp jobs, everybody had to be active. I personally chose to be in the team that cleaned the latrines, which was a very unpleasant job but only entailed two hours' work a day, so the rest of the day I was totally free to do whatever I liked: lie in the sun, read (we had a very good library), and generally amuse myself. It took me a while to get used to the latrine cleaning, but, well, it was just shit smell after all, and the fact that we could look forward to a free day after it was done made up for the rather onerous job of cleaning the shit out of the camp.

During the two years or more that we lived there, my sex life was dormant. I remember watching wrestling games between the boys; love affairs always started during these games on the parade ground. We had to have an early-morning parade and an evening parade to take a roll call, because there were some escape attempts, but of course there wasn't much to escape to, and the escapees were always roped in. They were easily recognizable by their accents. I never tried to escape, because I didn't think there was much point to it.

I was pretty fortunate, and of course I knew that one day, when the war had finished, we would be released. Although it was nerve-racking, because the war was going very badly for the Allies. We had a radio and followed the battles with great trepidation; communist or Jew, our sympathies were with the Allies.

During the summer evenings, when work was finished in the camp, we sat on our front steps or leaned against the wall and watched the world go by. A young boy whose name was Ossie was a part of this world. He used to wear the shortest shorts, very tight shirts, and little socks rolled down. He had beautiful legs. He was so round he looked like a pretty girl.

He was more or less the camp whore and used to get lots of favors from the guys that screwed him. Everybody whistled when he paraded down the camp streets, and he loved it. He was protected by someone in the camp government.

The toughest thing for me was that I was twenty years old, I'd been used to fucking regularly, and I badly missed the girls. There was no question of me turning homosexual—it didn't interest me.

Of course there was no alcohol allowed in the camp, but some of the more inventive inmates built stills and made a pretty potent kind of wine that was quite alcoholic, out of fruit or jam. We used to have parties, and people used to get drunk, but these stills had to be hidden very carefully. The only time that we were given alcohol was during Christmas or the New Year, which fall during the very hot season in Australia. They brought in a ration of beer. There wasn't much, but it was augmented by the secret stills.

We slept on wooden bedsteads with a wire base covered by a very rough palliasse filled with straw that could be renewed every month or so. We would go to the supply store and draw new straw. At the beginning of the month the straw was very hard and uncomfortable, and by the end of the month it was pretty painful, because it broke and used to stick into our asses and backs, poking right through the palliasse. It had a certain period of comfort, in the middle of the month, when it had just the perfect texture.

After drinking and eating, the homosexuals used to drag their beds and pillows out onto the parade ground. At Christmas and New Year's Eve, in the heat of the Australian night, the homosexual population of the camp embarked on a real Roman orgy under the stars. The couples were all over the parade ground.

We used to walk around to watch, and it was pretty exciting. The only relief that I, and people like me, got was masturbation, but we couldn't do it too much. I do remember one old guy who shared a hut with someone who eventually refused to keep sharing with him. The old guy was masturbating so much his roommate couldn't sleep at night. In the end, the great masturbator was shifted into a remote barracks where he could do whatever he wanted without disturbing anybody. This barracks was then referred to as "La Salle de la Masturbation."

What got me down was not knowing when we were going to get out. After two years, it was pretty depressing for a young man. I had arrived there when I was twenty years old, in 1940, and time seemed to drag on forever and ever, monotonously. To be without women, or any sort of outside contact, was pretty terrible for a young man. Some of the guys, the more adventurous ones, did cut into the fences and go into the single women's compound to fuck. They found plenty of willing women, who were pretty desperate too, for they were in the same boat as the guys. I was never amongst those that went through onto the other side. I had some mild flirtations through the fence, but that was all.

Lots of gifts arrived from the outside world; there was a Jewish Committee that used to send us books and stuff like that; there were the Quakers, the Society of Friends; there was the Salvation Army; and so on. I do remember one shipment that came from the Jewish Committee; it was an enormous shipment of clothes, and in it were a great number of tuxedos—

there were even some top hats. It was hilarious. The Salvation Army was very good; they used to send things that were useful, like toothpaste and toothbrushes. There was a canteen, and we could spend what was called camp money that was given to us by the authorities for certain jobs we did. It wasn't much, just pieces of cardboard with a stamp on them.

Some of the old Tatura inmates still have meetings in Melbourne and Sydney even today. They even bring out a roneoed Xeroxed newspaper. I have been sent copies, which I dispatched to the wastepaper basket very quickly, because I find this kind of living in the past useless and unproductive. I always have. When I started burning old photographs and old letters in Melbourne, before we left for Europe, June cried. It's something that I have always been obsessed with, throwing things away, traveling with as little baggage as possible, especially when I was young. I used to look forward to tomorrow, and I was never, ever interested in yesterday. Today was pretty good, and tomorrow could be even better.

So 1941 came around, and with it a change of Australian government. There had been a Conservative government before and now we had a Labour government under Prime Minister Curtin. These people looked at things in a more realistic way than the Conservatives. There was a great shortage of labor in Australia. All they had was a population of six million or something like that to defend this enormous continent. All the able-bodied men had been sent overseas, to the Middle East, to serve with the Allied forces, so there was nobody really left to do the work except women and old men and many Jews and communists that were bottled up in these internment camps.

The Labour government decided that, rather than let these people, these anti-Nazis, sit behind barbed wire, they might as well make us be useful to Australia and work for what they called the "war effort." A committee was set up that went into the internment camps to listen to each inmate's history, political or racial, and then declare who was safe to be let out and who was not. Of course, in our compound there was no problem at all—everybody was genuinely anti-Nazi.

However, as the war started to take a turn for the worse for Germany, the inmates of the Nazi internment camp asked the Australian authorities to send in a committee. They claimed to have been wrongly interned; they thought they should be in the anti-Nazi compounds. We're not Nazis, they said, we're anti-Nazis. We may not be Jewish, but we are anti-Nazis, and we have been wrongly put into this internment camp for Nazis.

Their claims to be anti-Nazis became more and more clamorous, and they became hysterical in their attempts to get out of that camp and join us in anti-Nazi Tatura One or Two, where they might find a safe haven for the future. So a commission came from Melbourne, and those who wanted to change their status from Nazi to anti-Nazi went before the commission, which consisted of a number of military officers and civilians.

One day our camp gates opened and admitted a small flood of young men who had come as transfers from those Nazi camps into ours. The rumors had spread that we would get a big transfer, and everybody, the whole camp population, was assembled at the barbed-wire cyclone-fencing gates to witness the arrival of the new inmates. The gates were opened by the Australian reservist soldiers, and a rather small detachment of young men walked in. We watched these guys come into our camp rather hesitantly, not knowing exactly what was going to happen to them. It was strange, it was quiet, there was no conversation. There were about two hundred of us watching just a few guys come in from the other camp.

Amongst the new arrivals I recognized three men. One was my old friend Peter Kaiser and one was Koslowsky, who had been caught with Peter by my father at my seventeenth-birthday party. The third was a guy whose name I didn't know but whose face I had seen before, I didn't know where. Later on I recognized him as the young storm trooper whom I had seen at the Halensee station in Berlin. His name was Hans Magulis, and his father had been stationed at the embassy in London.

One day I was told that a number of communists that were living with us had decided to string up Koslowsky and Kaiser, maybe some of the others as well. That same night I arranged to have a meeting with Peter to inform him of their intention. We met somewhere behind the barracks. It was quite dangerous for us to be seen together, and we risked being badly beaten up by the communists. Somebody must have gone to the Australian camp authorities and told them what was happening: a guard was posted by the barracks where these guys were living, and Peter and Koslowsky were attacked physically, but they were not killed.

One morning in the late summer of 1942, more than a year and a half after our arrival in Australia, we were told to pack our bags. My friend Wally and I stuck together, with some friends. We were a pretty tightly knit society, divided into groups whose members clung to each other. We were called to the camp gates, which opened to reveal a fleet of trucks waiting for us. No more camp guards, no more reservist Australian soldiers, but we didn't know where we were going.

The trucks took us to a town called Shepparton in Victoria, not very far away from Tatura. This was a very important place in Australia, the center of the fruit-and-canning industry, where miles and miles of fruit orchards, mostly peaches, were situated, together with big canning factories. It was an important part of the war effort to help in the harvesting of these peaches, with most of the able-bodied men being out of the country, and those who were left pretty old and decrepit.

They trucked us to the Shepparton Canning Factory, and in the yard we were unloaded and lined up in groups. We stuck together like mates clinging on to each other at a slave auction. We were lined up, and the local farmers appeared in their cars and confronted us.

It must have been a very strange sight for the Australians to see these aliens lined up. God knows how we were dressed, after two and a half years in the internment camp. We must have been a pretty grim sight.

On one side of the factory yard stood two hundred Jews of different ages—anything from eighteen or twenty to decrepit old Jews of fifty or more, professors, teachers, doctors, writers, and musicians, all this intellectual flotsam and jetsam from Berlin that had washed up on the factory yard in Shepparton—and opposite these two hundred guys, about fifty Australian fruit-growers from the Shepparton area looking for a workforce to do the harvesting in their fruit orchards.

They walked amongst our ranks, taking a good look at our physical condition, particularly feeling the muscles of our arms. They weren't interested in the fifty- or sixty-year-old professors or teachers, doctors or dentists, they were interested in guys like me and my mates, young ones that looked healthy enough to do the picking.

These guys looked very different from anything I'd ever seen before. They wore wide-brimmed hats, and they spoke in a broad Australian dialect that I couldn't understand. Wally and I huddled together with our group of friends. Our greatest fear was to be separated, but, as luck had it, we all stayed together. I think there were five or six of us. We were taken away in a truck to a big fruit orchard in the vicinity of Shepparton.

Peaches were graded for size on grading tables that had a very strong slant. The fruit would run around down various channels and fall into holes made for the different sizes of peach. We were told we could sleep in the grading sheds. There was hay around, and it was more than uncomfortable, although certainly nothing like as luxurious as Tatura Internment Camp. On the first night, it was very cold—the days were hot and the nights were freezing. We tried to sleep on the ground, but there was too much stuff crawling around: insects, spiders, and snakes. Snakes are very prevalent in Australia, and they're all poisonous. Wally and I got pretty scared, so we climbed onto the grading table and tried to sleep on that hard wooden surface. With the very strong slant, you had to hang on with one arm so as not to roll off. Trying to get a night's sleep like that was pretty nightmarish.

The farmer had a daughter whose name was Sunshine. We were not allowed to go to the front door of the house, we were only allowed to go to the back door. She used to give us scraps to eat from the kitchen. On Sundays, Sunshine would come to the shed with a great big bowl of stewed peaches, because that's the only thing anybody ate. There were raw peaches, stewed peaches, and most of all there were tinned stewed peaches. I couldn't look at a peach for many years afterwards. We got quite friendly with the farmer, and as Wally was a good musician (he had a violin and an accordion with him), we were often invited into the house. We'd sit down in the living room, and Wally would entertain us on the piano, or sometimes he would play the fiddle or whatever was handy, and everybody would sing around the piano. I remember the farmer saying to Wally and all of us assembled there, "Ah, you see, just like fruit picking, the fiddle is just like fruit picking, once you get the knack of it it's just like playing the bloody fiddle."

We got used to the Australian idiom. Very early in our relationship with Sunshine's father, somebody referred to him as a "wag." Now, I didn't know what a wag was, and neither did Wally so we said, "Wag, what's a wag?" Oh, he's a bit of a wag—did that mean that he would whip us, did it mean he would maltreat us? We didn't know what a wag was. We didn't know what he had in store for us.

In the end, it became impossible for us to sleep in the grading shed, so the farmer informed us that we were welcome to go and camp in an empty house that belonged to him half a mile away. There was nobody there, so Wally and I picked up our belongings and installed ourselves in that house.

One night there was a terrible banging on the door. We unlocked it, and some Albanians came in with drawn knives. They said that it was their house and that they wanted to take possession of it. We pulled on our underpants, gathered our clothes, and ran across the fields. It was a terrible night, pitch black, and we fell down into the gutters by the side of the road as we stumbled back into Sunshine's father's shed.

Soon afterwards, the farmer went to the house and with the help of his mates got rid of the Albanians. This time it was their turn to flee. He told us that we could move back in, although a couple of guys who were working on another orchard were staying there too, seasonal laborers. But there was plenty of room in the house for all of us, so there would be no problem.

The two guys were living in one of the rooms across the passage from us with a girl who did the cooking. They were Australian illiterates. The girl wasn't bad-looking. This was not long after we had been released from Tatura, and we hadn't had any kind of sexual contact with girls for over two years. We hadn't been in Shepparton town very much, because we were so tired after fruit picking that we just fell into whatever our places of rest were and passed out.

Fruit picking started early in the morning, when it was freezing, but by midday it was boiling hot. There were a lot of spider's webs in the orchards. Australian spiders are a pretty dangerous lot; there are very few species that are not poisonous. I remember seeing a beautiful spider's web in the morning, covered with the early-morning dew, whilst enormous spiders climbed up and down it. I was shit-scared. Everything was threatening—the spiders in trees and, between trees, the snakes underfoot.

Once I was walking over fallen leaves in the orchard when I stood on something quite hard and it jumped up. I was sure it was a snake, and I screamed and made a step backwards, but this thing jumped up again. It was a branch that I'd stood on, but it scared the shit out of me. It was early morning, there wasn't much light, and I was sure I'd trodden on the tail of a snake. I still remember it like it was yesterday.

You had to be very careful what you picked in the orchard, because the peaches had to have a certain ripeness and color. One of our mates, Harry Jeidels, was up on the ladder picking away with sunglasses on, so he only picked green peaches. When Sunshine's father came through the orchard checking his laborers, he threw a fit when he saw this guy on top of the ladder picking peaches with his sunglasses on. He shouted up: "Come down here, you, you bastard, let me have a look in your bag"—because we wore bags across our shoulders into which we used to put the peaches that we had picked. Once the bag was full, we'd come down the ladder and put them into the fruit cases. So big, fat Harry came waddling down the ladder to have his bag inspected. He still had the sunglasses on his nose, and of course the boss found nothing but green peaches in the bloody bag. So the boss ripped the sunglasses off Harry's nose and said, "You bastard, never wear those sunglasses again while you work here. You won't get a penny for today's work!"

When the rains came there was no fruit picking at all, because you can't pick peaches when they are wet, and I remember we had quite a few rainy days. We didn't get paid if we didn't work: we got paid by the case of peaches that we picked. They were counted and stacked in the orchards and we were paid accordingly for piecework, so we didn't have anything to eat. We had no money. We went from farmhouse to farmhouse, pulling our caps, knocking at the back door asking for work, whatever work was offered. I could drive a truck, Wally could always play the fiddle, and sometimes we got odd work and it kept us in bread and jam. Bread was cheap, and jam was cheap because we were in the heart of the canning country. When the sun came out we went back to picking peaches.

The only thing that was wonderful was having one's friends with one. We were all in the same boat. We used to laugh an awful lot, because they were so strange to us, the Australians. I remember when we came down the road we used to see the Aussies coming toward us, going for walks or going to work, and we'd made up the conversation before we passed them. We knew the platitudes; the exchange was totally predictable. For instance, they'd say, "Good morning, how you going? Hot enough for you? Doing all right?" And we made up all these answers and questions in advance. It never failed, the platitudes were always the same, their questions were the same, the answers were the same.

Now, back to the house in which we were living. The two guys with their girlfriend were living in the room on the right, Wally and I in the room on the left. We became a little bit friendly, and after the second or third night we had our supper with them. Afterwards we were climbing into our beds when there was a rap on the door, and one of the guys came into our room and said to me: "How would you like to have a go at my sheila?" Well, this seemed to be an incredible God-given opportunity, so I hopped out of bed and followed the guy into his room across the landing; there on the floor the girl was curled up with the other guy on a big mattress with a few pillows. She made a welcoming gesture to me. She was pretty good-looking, and at least at the time I thought she was fantastic. I just flew into bed. I didn't take any notice of her friend next to her and started to fuck her.

We had a wonderful time, but a few minutes later the other guy, who had brought me into the room, jumped into bed—that made a sandwich with his friend on the left of the girl and me and the other one on her other side. Obviously what he wanted to do was to bugger me, and he already had me in a clinch with my back to him. He was stark naked. I just let out a blood-curdling scream. I don't know how I got out of his clutches, because I'm not very strong and these guys were all muscle and didn't muck about, but in desperation I jumped out of bed and raced across into mine and Wally's room, locked the door, and just crawled under the bedsheets. That was my first sexual encounter after Tatura.

We went down to Shepparton from time to time, especially to the local dances on Saturday nights, but the natives did not take kindly to us. First of all, the local girls were very intrigued by us. They had never seen a foreigner. You mustn't forget that this was 1942 in Australia, a tiny population in a small town on this enormous continent. There were hardly any foreigners in Australia at the time; there were a few Greeks who had some restaurants, and some Chinese greengrocers, but that was about it. Foreigners of our kind had never been seen before. The girls were interested in us, but the local guys were up in arms against us, and so were the politicians. I remember one Member of Parliament, a guy called Joe Gullett, who wrote in a weekly newspaper called *The Truth*—a truly scandalous right-wing, fascist, anti-everything newspaper, full of gossip and scandal, that everybody read. (I mean, June's family read it—there wasn't a household in Australia that did not get *The Truth* on a Friday night.)

Anyway, Gullett wrote in *The Truth*: "There are foreigners treading our pavements in the town of Shepparton, ogling our girls." The Saturday night after this article appeared, meaning the next evening, we went downtown as usual, because we didn't know anything about *The Truth* and we didn't read the newspapers. There was a whole gang of local Shepparton louts waiting for us, waiting to beat us up, so we just took to our heels and ran back to the orchard.

Some Saturday nights, when we had enough money in our pockets and we felt like some luxury, Wally and I used to take a room in the Shepparton Hotel. It was a room with old furniture, in a sort of Victorian hotel. It was quite beautiful; there was an enormous double bed in it, and we used to have a hot bath and have dinner in the dining room. Of course we had no girls, because of Gullett and the local lads, so we were just the two of us. We'd gorge ourselves with food in the hotel restaurant and then stay forever in the bathtub and a have good sleep in a real bed.

After a couple of months or so, the fruit-picking season was over and we were told to go down to Melbourne. By that time we had a little bit of money, enough to take the train, and they said: "Well, you can volunteer for the army. If you don't volunteer for the army, you know what we're gonna do with you, we're gonna put you back into the camp." Right from the beginning, from the slave market in the yard of the Shepparton Canning Factory, our employers had always had this whip over us. They used to say, "If you don't work properly, we'll send you back to internment, back to the camp at Tatura." Of course we were shit-scared that that's exactly what was going to happen, and the one thing we didn't want to do was to go back. I don't know what the alternative to not volunteering was—I'm sure there was something—but the army sounded a lot more attractive to me and to my friends, so we took the train to Melbourne. We had to report to Flemington Racecourse, where they had established an army-induction center.

CHAPTER FIVE

THE ARMY, 1942–1946

I GOT OUT at Flinders Street Station—which every Australian had assured me was the world's busiest railway station—and walked out onto the main road. It was a gray day, and all of a sudden I burst into tears. I'd never been so sad in my life. I'd never seen anything quite as ugly as Flinders Street.

I just walked along with the tears streaming down my face. Thank God, this kind of depression didn't last long. I reported to Flemington Racecourse with all my friends, and in true Australian fashion everything was very relaxed. The induction into the army was very low-key. We had to be on the racecourse, which was treated like a parade ground, every morning, so our names could be called, and then we were told that we had the day off, that we didn't have to come back until the evening. The Australians didn't quite know what to do with us. They knew they wanted to use us, that they needed a labor force, but they hadn't worked out exactly how they should go about it.

Eventually, we were inducted into the army and slept on Flemington Racecourse. It was pretty primitive, but certainly better than the stables in Shepparton. Many of our friends disappeared for days on end. I had some

Austrian friends who were avid skiers. They got themselves some girlfriends and went up to the mountains of Victoria to ski, and they were never missed. They just ambled back into Flemington Racecourse and stood on the parade ground. When their names were called they would say: "Present, sir," and that was it.

I stuck with Wally and another close friend of mine, Philip Krems, who was Viennese. We were very close friends. In prewar times, Philip had been a very ambitious officer in the Austrian cavalry. When it was discovered that he was half or quarter Jewish, he was thrown out of the cavalry and ended up immigrating to Australia. We had met in Singapore and become friends in Tatura, and the friendship had developed even further in Melbourne.

After our induction on Flemington Racecourse, we were quartered in a very big army camp on the outskirts of Melbourne called Camp Pell, five minutes' tram ride from the center of the city, where at last we were let loose on the local girls. This was no Shepparton. It was a wild scene for us. We truly fucked ourselves silly.

Life was very easy. One girlfriend replaced another. I met a wonderful Irish Catholic girl with flaming-red hair. Her name was Mary Flanagan. She had one brother working in the Richmond Beer Brewery, and another brother in the Carreras cigarette factory, which made Craven A. Of course, in those days, beer and cigarettes were hard to come by, very severely rationed, and Mary used to supply me with everything. She was also wonderful in another way. She never wanted to go to a movie, she never wanted to go out, she just wanted to go up into our room and fuck.

The only trouble was that she was a true child of the people. Her English was basic, to say the least, and grammatically incorrect. When we were in bed together she would talk while we were fucking and she would say "You was" instead of "You were," and make other grammatical mistakes. I had to ask her, "Please, please, Mary, do not speak while we are fucking, because I like it better if we don't." Of course, I much prefer it if people do speak in bed, but the snobby young Helmut just couldn't bear to listen to those ungrammatical sentences. Every time she said "You was" and similar, my erection would disappear and I would become completely impotent.

A lot of refugees had arrived from all over Europe. Amongst them there was a very good-looking Polish countess and her husband, who must have come with quite a lot of money, because they established themselves in an old Victorian house on St. Kilda Road, which was a beautiful residential quarter in Melbourne.

She entertained the guys from the army corps frequently, and her husband was never much in evidence. We had wild parties at the countess's house. There were quite exotic stories about how she got to Australia, how she and her husband had escaped from Poland to Australia. I had a rip-roaring affair with her and very soon found out that I was just one of many from our army company. Phil was one of the other lovers, and he and I used to compare notes on her.

I remember she had a big cunt. She must have been fucking for a long time, and it was difficult to fuck her because there was a minimum of friction. Philip and I and a few other guys exchanged all these technical, intimate details, and we had a wonderful time comparing notes. Don't forget we were young blades; we were really going hell for leather.

When Josette's sister, Kitty, turned up in Melbourne (her husband, Dick, had joined the Allied forces), she installed herself in a comfortable flat. This was my opportunity to make up for lost time. We had a wild affair. It was winter, and she used to receive me wearing a fur coat and be stark naked under it, then she would take it off and spread it on the ground, and we would fuck in front of the fireplace. Sometime later, I introduced her to my friend Philip, who took her fancy, and she had him on alternate nights. When I was with her she would describe her lovemaking with Philip in great detail: Philip had ambitions in the army, and soon became a lance corporal, ending up as a sergeant, and felt patriotic as an Australian soldier, whereas I had never had these ambitions, was happy to stay a buck private and just have fun. Anyway, Kitty told me that while they were fucking the radio was always turned on playing music, and at the end of the program "God Save the King" was always played, and Philip used to jump out of bed, stand to attention, and salute, then jump right back and continue fucking.

I asked Kitty what had happened to Josette, and Kitty told me that she was in a prison camp. She didn't even know if Josette was alive or not. I asked her why Josette hadn't come with her, and she said, "She didn't want to come."

Many years later, in the 1960s, I was having afternoon tea in the lobby of the Piccadilly Hotel in London with June and an actor friend of hers when I was paged. A Miss Van Doyle was asking for me. It was Kitty's daughter—the little girl I used to take by the hand in the parks and gardens of Singapore and walk up and down so that the adults could talk.

She had turned into a buxom, bosomy wench, and here indeed was an opportunity to complete the circle, if only June hadn't been there. June later told me that the actor friend had said that her presence certainly put a damper on an otherwise very promising situation.

Philip and I decided that we were going to rent, very cheaply, a room in a suburb called South Yarra. We called it "Schloss Rammelfeste," after a famous nineteenth-century Austrian pornographic novel. "Rammelfeste" means "fuck hard"; we referred to our room as "Castle Fuck Hard." We would take our respective girlfriends back there and fuck away and have a great time drinking wine and trying to make up for lost time in Tatura.

The army service, for the time being, was pretty good. I had learned how to do a minimum of work. Walk around the camp listlessly and without any purpose and some sergeant would haul you in to work. He would give you some kind of kitchen duty, KP or whatever, or you'd have to clean something, anything. I wasn't very keen on that. There was too much time to be made up, and too much fun to be had in town. So I developed a way of looking purposeful and walking purposefully. I always had a big ruler in my hand, or three pieces of timber and a hammer, and I would walk around the camp without anything to do but looking like a man with a mission. Saluting smartly all passing officers in true Prussian fashion. They loved it.

We had a commanding officer called Captain Broughton, a Maori, a big war hero from the First World War, a fine figure of a man. He was very proud to have this ramshackle band of intellectual and artistic soldiers who were going to be great in battle. He tried his utmost to get to what was called in those days "up north." "Up north" was where the Japs were, "up north" was where the real battle was. Of course, the last thing that any of us wanted to do was to go "up north"; it would have been the end of us. Then the sad day came and the order was given for the platoon to be shipped out of Melbourne. We were to be sent up north, but not very far, only something like five hundred kilometers, just over the Victoria–New South Wales border, into this little township of Tocumwal.

Captain Broughton was a romantic person who was full of fancy ideas. The fact that he thought his boys were going to become great war heroes and a great battalion of fighters shows you what kind of romantic he was. Anyway, this order was posted on the bulletin board, and one night, soon after I was asleep in my tent in Camp Pell, dreaming away, I felt a hand on my shoulder, shaking me. I sleep very deeply, and I dream, so when somebody wakes me I jump out of my skin and start screaming. I shot out of bed and threw my arms around the neck of the person who was shaking me, and of course it was Captain Broughton.

He said, "Driver Neustaedter, don't be scared, it's only your commanding officer, it's your captain." I let him go and said, "Yes, sir. Yes, sir," and he said, "Get dressed, we will leave under cover of darkness." There was no enemy lurking in the streets of Melbourne or on the road to Tocumwal, but it sounded better to say that he and his driver (that was me) were leaving under cover of night to establish camp up north, in little Tocumwal, across the border, by a river.

So I got into my uniform and packed my kit bag with all my belongings— which weren't very many, a few books and whatever—and threw them into the truck. Wally Würzburger was there too, because he was the camp bugler and musician. They had a good regimental band, having all those Jewish musicians who had played in God knows what places in Europe, coffeehouses or concert halls or whatever. They loaded up some drums and instruments, then Wally Würzburger, Captain Broughton, plus his driver Helmut set off under cover of darkness.

I had been woken out of such a deep sleep that I wasn't all there. We got out onto the highway, which was a pretty terrible road between Melbourne and Albury. Albury was the last main town before you hit the River Murray, which marked the border of New South Wales and Victoria. It was pitch black, and Wally was wrapped up in three or four army blankets, shivering in

the back. All the instruments were there. I was driving, Captain Broughton was sitting next to me, and of course I fell asleep.

We ended up in a big ditch by the side of the road. All the instruments and drums had fallen out and rolled over the field. Nobody was hurt, thank God. Then we had to push the truck out of the ditch, and Wally and I had to find all the instruments, which were strewn all over the road and the field, while Captain Broughton sat there waiting for us to load it all back up. Eventually, we arrived in Tocumwal.

Captain Broughton established us in our new quarters in Tocumwal, which was a lovely camp and not far from the river. It was a really wonderful place, set in beautiful Australian countryside with great big eucalyptus trees, which the Australians call "gum trees." A tiny little township, with one main drag, a great number of churches, and an even bigger number of pubs. We were attached to another company. The new commanding officer had about five hundred guys under his command, and we were attached to his company to work in Tocumwal on the railroads.

I remember Captain Broughton making a speech to the platoon before we left Camp Pell: "Boys, whatever you do, don't lose your identity. You belong to the Eighth Corps, don't you forget you belong to the Eighth Corps."

And there we were, under the rules and regulations of this commanding officer who was commanding five hundred Greeks, a rough-and-ready lot who were pretty aggressive and who didn't get on with us at all. The captain in charge of the Greeks hated this new detachment that had come to Tocumwal; he hated us. But Captain Broughton had done us a very good deal, he had appointed Lieutenant Thomas to the cushy job of looking after these intellectual Yids, after having fought in the desert with the Australian army.

Curly Thomas—as he was known in true Australian fashion, because he was as bald as an egg—was a really sweet guy, and a great drinker and womanizer. The last thing he was interested in was doing any work or having anything to do with the administration of his platoon.

As in any military camp, we had a big parade ground and a morning and

evening roll call. The roll calls were always taken by the lieutenant; the captain would just come onto the parade ground at the last minute, salute, and walk off again. As I was the company driver, I had a very special duty. My duty was to find Curly—who would be getting drunk in town—just before the evening roll call. It would take me about an hour to make the rounds of all the pubs—there were eight or ten of them—until I found Lieutenant Curly and flushed him out of the pub, dead drunk. I would load him into my truck and deliver him to the sergeant major so that he would be there, standing on the parade ground, to take the salute on the hour, and to salute the commanding officer. This was one of my most important duties.

The Australian army was fantastic; there was absolutely no formality, it was very laissez-faire, and there was a very good relationship between Curly and his courageous troops. As I have already said, he was a great womanizer, and there were many evenings during the week when he would say to me, "Come on, Helmut, back up to the back door of the canteen and load up three blankets and a crate of beer." Then we'd go to the dances in the neighboring township, called Cobram. In Cobram there was a big air-force hospital with a lot of air-force nurses, and there were a lot of dances there, in the Cobram Mechanics Institute Hall.

Cobram was a very pretty little town; the streets were lined with trees; it was a little bit Wild West. Curly would pick up a nurse and he'd say, "Helmut, pick yourself a nurse." He never liked the idea of fucking if I had nothing to do by his side, or was waiting in the truck. He was happier if I too had something to occupy my time. So I'd try to find a nice nurse, and the four of us would set off to the banks of the Murray or somewhere in the countryside and spread the blankets. I would bring out the beer, and Curly would be ten or fifteen yards away, fucking with his nurse, and when everything was finished we'd deliver the nurses back to the RAAF hospital. On the way back to camp, Curly would be very solicitous, asking me, "Did you have a good time? How did the fucking go? What was she like? Give me the details," and then he would give me the details of his night. The spirit was fantastic, it was just great.

The reason we were in Tocumwal was that on the border of Victoria and New South Wales there was what was called a "break of gauge." In those days (1943–44), every state in the Commonwealth of Australia had a different-sized gauge railway. This meant that the train from Melbourne would arrive at the border, just outside of Albury, and everything—passengers, goods, and so on—had to be transferred from the Victoria train onto the New South Wales train, because neither one nor the other could use the rail of the other state. We were there to transfer all the goods from one train to the other.

This was done manually. There were no cranes. It was very badly organized. We had to be out there in the heat all day long. Being smart Yids, we had a meeting and decided we suggest to the officers that we work much more efficiently but much shorter hours.

The two sets of truck doors would be opened, and then two or three planks would be put across between them, like a little bridge, and the goods would be transferred from one freight truck to the other. This was done by a gang of five. Two guys stayed and loaded the goods onto the back of one guy, who would go over the little wooden bridge and would put the load down. Then there was another guy, standing on the other side, who would move it into its place, so he could get as much freight into one truck as possible. Most of the goods were perishable, like potatoes and onions. I think they were in fifty-pound or hundred-pound bags. They had to be stacked in a certain way—five over the gunnel or six over the gunnel, we called it—so that they would not fall off and would stay perfectly steady once the train was in motion.

There was quite an art to it, and we mastered it pretty smartly. What we proposed to the officers was the following: A gang of five could move fifty tons every day. So we would move fifty tons of goods a day in whatever time and order we chose. Fifty tons is quite a lot, but if we took all day it didn't matter; it was left to us as loaders and carriers to see how efficiently we could work. We did our fifty tons of goods in something like three hours. After that, we had the rest of the day free.

The weather was beautiful. You could lie in the sun, you could go into town, get drunk, do all kinds of things. It worked for the masters and it worked for us. It was efficient. I remember there was also some civilian labor. There were two brothers, one was about seventy and the other one was sixty-eight, and the older one would refer to his sixty-eight-year-old brother as "me kid brother."

So the township of Tocumwal became something like home. We got on extremely well with the locals, we became very friendly with them. The fact that we were in an Australian uniform made all the difference in the world. We were accepted. We were invited into their homes, and after the war three or four guys in my company married the daughters of very rich people in Tocumwal.

We did the same job in the bigger town, Albury, where we were stationed for a while, again to work on the railroads. On one side of Albury Station there was a freight siding, and on the other side there was a siding for passenger trains. In those days there was one train which was laughingly referred to as a "crack train" between Melbourne and Albury, called the *Spirit of Progress*. It was a passenger train, and quite luxurious and fast for those days.

When we were working at night, which was quite often, we used to wait for the *Spirit of Progress* to come in. We had a very good trick. We would wait where the dining car pulled up, and where waiters from the dining car would be all ready, standing in the open door with brown paper bags full of leftovers from the passengers' dinners. They used to sell them to us for very little, and it was very good food—chicken legs, all kinds of delicious things. We lived like kings. We used to take the bags back to the camp and make great suppers of that excellent food, together with a lot of beer. The cuisine of the *Spirit of Progress,* bought at two or three shillings a brown paper bag, was a good deal.

I remember it as if it were yesterday, standing on the platform of Albury Station with two or three friends of mine, waiting for the train to pull in, and knowing exactly where the dining car would stop.

In Albury I had a girlfriend called Leslie. She was a schoolteacher. She was a very nice girl, blonde and tall. She used to take me home to her mother's for a good meal. The mother thought it was wonderful for her daughter to be exposed to the cultural influence of a real European, who could teach her so many interesting things from the other side of the world. Of course, all the European had in his head was trying to get Leslie into bed and fuck the ass off her. Leslie proved to be a hard nut to crack, though she was very sweet and loved me dearly.

We spent hours kissing and lying in the grass, but I can't remember whether it ever came to the crunch. But it was very nice, and the meals that her mother made were excellent. My cultural influence was great, and I'm sure that, even if I didn't make what we called in those days a home run, I still had a very good time.

Also in Albury there was a steak-and-egg joint. Steak and eggs was the Australians' staple diet. I remember going there at night and having a pass-word, "steak upstairs," which meant that there were girls up on the first floor that we could fuck. Those days in Albury offered an extraordinary introduc-tion to Australian lore and culture. We really fitted into the community, and the people were lovely.

One working party in Melbourne that was very popular with me and my mates was the Footscray Canning Factory. We loved going there, because there were a lot of women, and they were pretty rough and tough. At lunchtime we would fuck some of them behind the stacks of boxes filled with cans. It was nice. It was very nice.

I also worked on a working party in the CSR, the Colonial Sugar Refinery, where I drove a winch loading bags of sugar. I used to have two weeks of headaches from the smell of the sugar. It was unbelievably hard work. It was hot, it was summer, and the fumes coming off the sugar were unbearable.

Then there was another working party—unloading the cement ships from America. It was done by manpower alone. We were sent down to Port Melbourne for two weeks to unload these big bags of cement. The ships were never-ending. I remember for two weeks I was white, because the cement used to set under the shower and you couldn't wash it off. This was when the scare was on that the Japanese would invade Australia. America saved Australia from the Japanese invasion, because there weren't enough Australian soldiers left at home. Most of them were fighting in the Far East and Middle East.

Toward the end of the war, I changed my room to a little hut at the back of a rooming house in Bromby Street, South Yarra, a suburb of Melbourne. When I say a "little hut," it was truly a little hut, under a big old tree, with a kind of car port at the back of it where I later kept my car. It was about two meters wide and four meters long. As you came in, my cabin trunk, which I had brought all the way from Berlin, stood in the left-hand corner.

There were some little photographs and some framed collages that I had done as a young boy hanging on the walls. The walls were covered with faded floral wallpaper, and there was a very narrow single iron bedstead covered with a faded floral cotton bedspread. It also had a washstand with a mirror above it. And that was about it, because you couldn't fit anything more in.

The only door was what the Australians call a "fly-wire door"—a screen door. To have a shower, I had to go into the main house, which meant going across a pretty backyard with flowers, into the house, along a corridor, and into the only bathroom in the boarding house. The people who had large rooms there (it was an old Australian house) were not paupers, but there was only one bathroom, and when it was taken, which it often was, I had to go all the way back down the corridor, through the garden, wait for a while, and then go all the way back to the bathroom. I needed shilling pieces for the bath heater, to light the gas, which used to start with an enormous bang.

I used to take all my girls back to my little green hut. Amongst them I remember a fabulous girl called Betty. She was a very sexy girl, with the tiniest waist and great big breasts. We had a rip-roaring affair and used to fuck away in the little green hut like nobody's business. I had stolen Betty from her boyfriend, Jack. On a number of occasions he would creep up behind the little hut. It was very easy to get into the backyard: you just came in the front gate and walked around the house.

As we were fucking away on my narrow single bed, I would hear rustling in the bushes behind the hut and I would say to Betty, "Quiet, quiet, Jack is there," and then Jack would scream, "I know you're in there, Betty, come out, I know that Helmut is fucking you!" Sometimes I would just get up and scream, "Get the fuck out of here!" I think he got bored with all that, because he disappeared, but eventually Betty went back to Jack and they got married.

I had another girlfriend, one of the few, if not the only, Jewish girlfriends

I ever had. Her name was Louise Golding, and she came from a rich family. Her father had a manufacturing business that stamped gold letters onto leatherbound books. She was a wild fuck, fabulous.

She had something that I have never encountered in any other woman. She had a bone placed somewhere, just above her vagina, that gave me a very special sensation while I was fucking her. Sometimes it hurt me, because she always responded quite wonderfully. She was a very nice girl, and I was really fond of her. At one moment of terrible weakness, I proposed to her, and I was taken up immediately, without any hesitation whatsoever. I sometimes went to her house for dinner, because, as it was a good Jewish house, the food was excellent and her mother cooked very well. I didn't go too often, because it bored the shit out of me. Actually, I can't remember whether I proposed or whether she proposed, but if she did, like a fool I said yes. Immediately I was taken home for dinner, and Louise announced that we were engaged at the dinner table.

I died at this dinner with the family, because the father took me aside and said, "You won't have any worries, my boy, because we're well off and you're going to go into the business." When I came home after the dinner, I couldn't sleep. I didn't sleep for nights on end.

The war was just about finished, and things in the army had become even more relaxed than they were during wartime, but I still had to stay in the army, because discharge from the Australian army was on a points system. Which meant that a guy who was not married and who didn't have any kids or any family was about the last one to be discharged. I had a very good time. I had it easy. I didn't have to work hard. Finally, in 1946, I was discharged.

In 1946, again driven by the ambition to become a famous photographer, I decided to change my name. Neustaedter didn't sound right for the new personage that I had in mind. It was like shedding a skin, a project that sounded adventurous to me, like leaving the Foreign Legion with a new identity. I decided this person would still have ties to his early youth, so I'd keep my first name Helmut and chose Newton, which seemed a good translation from Neustaedter. I swore never to think of myself as Neustaedter again. Although a few people suspected that this was not my real name, I was very successful in convincing the world that I was Helmut Newton. When the Australian government offered me its passport, I eagerly accepted, having spent all those first happy years in the country. When asked what city I chose as my birthplace, I did not hesitate to say "Berlin." That way, my past was to become real but also somewhat contradictory.

③

Registrar-General's Office,

Melbourne, 4ᵗʰ December 1946

DEPOSITED by *H. Newton Esq.*
in this Office, in pursuance of Section 15 of Property Law Act 1928, the following Documents :—

No. 18690   DEED POLL evidencing CHANGE OF NAME

from

Helmut Neustaedter

to

Helmut Newton

Crawford McAluce

Deputy Registrar-General.

One document,

CHAPTER SIX
MELBOURNE, 1946–1956

I CAN REMEMBER the great euphoria I felt when I was discharged from the army in 1946. They gave me a hundred pounds, which they called "deferred pay." I raced around with that hundred pounds in my hot

little hand and bought myself this beautiful car, a Ford V8 four-door tourer built in 1930, straight out of *The Untouchables*. Now I was once more penniless, like in Singapore after visiting that bordello.

My mother, who was living with my brother in the Argentine, wrote to me and said that she'd like me to join them there (my father had passed away). I wrote back and said, "It's out of the question. I love Australia. I wouldn't dream of going to South America. I wouldn't dream of going anywhere else. I want to stay here. I'm happy here. I adore the people. I love the country."

I opened my tiny studio in Melbourne in 1946. I found this penthouse in Flinders Lane where I paid a monthly rent of five Australian pounds.

I never thought I'd make any money, because when I started in photography people didn't make money. If you want to make money, don't become a photographer, because the odds are you won't. You might make a good living if you're lucky, but you're never going to have real money.

I was never interested in having an office or a staff. I hated the idea. I've always been a lone wolf and have only worked with one assistant. Nothing much has changed today. Still no studio, just one office, one secretary, one assistant.

A girl who worked part-time as my retoucher had a girlfriend who was an actress. She suggested to her that she come to see me to pick up some modeling work to make a little cash on the side. She came into the front office of my studio. There was nobody there; I didn't have a secretary, it was just me, and I was busy in the darkroom or something. So she sat herself down and studied the photographs displayed on the walls of my tiny office. And that was June.

She told me later that she had never seen anything like them. She was totally fascinated and expected "Helmut Newton" to be an old man with a long beard. And then I opened the door and stuck my head through, and it wasn't "an old man with a long beard," but this dashing foreign photographer!

So, because she was very pretty, I immediately said, "You must come for test photographs," as all photographers do, even today. Young photographers,

if they want to lay the model, say, "Come for test shots after working hours." And so she came, but I didn't get anywhere.

So I asked her for a date to take her out for dinner, and she said she liked the idea. I took her to a restaurant in Melbourne called Mario's, which was pretty expensive. As we sat there, over our first dinner, in my mind I was counting the money in my pocket, which wasn't very much.

And when we came to dessert, June looked at the menu and decided that she wanted crêpe Suzette. She didn't even know what the fuck crêpe Suzette was, but it was the most expensive thing on the menu. She swears to me that she didn't see the price, that she just liked the idea of eating crêpe Suzette. I said to myself, "The bitch. She chooses the most expensive dessert on the menu, and I'm worrying if I'll have enough money in my pocket to pay for the dinner."

On weekends I took June out to the countryside, in my beautiful car that

I'd lovingly baptized "Veronica," for picnics of chicken and beer. I think I bought the chicken. Once we'd found a good spot, we'd spread a blanket and have our picnic, then I'd try to get the clothes off her, and I'd kiss her, which she liked very much. She had a lot of boyfriends. I remember she used to wear a beautiful white sweater that had the names of boys embroidered all over it. This sweater was jam-packed with boys' names. There was Gaston, there was Bill, there was David, there was I don't know who, but I, never having been jealous, wasn't worried at all. I thought it was very amusing.

I didn't get very far with her. I sort of got excited, then I got mad, because I'm European and I don't go in for this kind of "cock teasing." It was just that she didn't want to get laid.

Eventually, I laid her in my little hut.

And then we decided to go away for a few days to an old mining town called Ballarat, a few hours from Melbourne, to test our compatibility. We checked into an hotel and spent the night together on a squeaky iron bed with a dreadful mattress. How satisfactory can a fucking session be as a night of passion on a bed like that? So that wasn't too good, but it didn't stop us, and we decided it was going to get better all the time, which of course it did.

I was still dating Louise at the same time. I was dating quite a lot of girls. I had my old girlfriend Dora McLennan, who had been my girlfriend during the war years. Although we didn't fuck anymore, or not very often anyway, we had stayed very good friends. She was an intelligent woman, much older than me. She was working in a laboratory for industrial chemical analysis on Flinders Lane. Her boss was an ex-lover of hers. She had had a great number of lovers in the past. Later on she had a lover who used to beat her up a lot. That was at the time when I was still seeing her, and I think she liked being beaten up. Anyway, her boss was a very nice guy, and sometimes I used to go up to her office and we'd go out and have lunch and the boss would come along too.

Although my English was perfectly fluent, Dora's boss knew I was a foreigner, and so he used to shout at me, because he always thought that I would understand better if he spoke very loudly. So he screamed at me over lunch; it was funny. The conversation was at such high volume on his side that Dora would say, "Stop shouting at him. He speaks very good English! He understands English!"

At some stage, I became quite serious about June and started thinking about possibly marrying her, but of course I was already engaged to Louise. I was in a terrible quandary, and I rang Dora when it was at a critical point and said, "Listen, come and have lunch with me, I need your advice." So I told her the situation I was in, and her advice was perfect. She said, "Well, tell me this. You really want to marry June?" I said, "Well, I'm not sure yet, but I think I might."

She said, "Is Louise pregnant?" I said, "No, of course not!" and she said, "Well, what's your problem? Just tell her it's all off!" Very good advice, as sensible as ever. I always have the highest regard for women's intelligence and cool-headedness.

So June and I went steady. She suited me perfectly as a girlfriend, for the simple reason that she worked in the theater at night. During the day she worked in an office. The department head must have liked her very much, or I don't know why he ever put up with her—she never did anything. She used to learn her lines under the desk during the day for the plays she performed at night.

So I became a stage-door Johnny. At night I printed in my darkroom, and at 9 p.m. I went straight to the theater and sat in the back row and saw the play June was acting in, over and over again. I mean, every night. I was totally fascinated by it. We'd all go to supper after the show. Then I'd drive her all the way home to her suburban house in the genteel suburb of Canterbury.

During the day, I would walk down Flinders Lane, the long, narrow street where all the rag traders were, showing my pictures and trying to get work, hoping for a break as a fashion photographer.

After an outing to the country or the movies with one's girlfriend, it was the custom to be "invited in" for tea or supper, depending on the time of day or night, but June never did. Then I found out the reason: she couldn't make a cup of tea. She didn't even know how to boil a kettle. When she finally invited me into the house, her mother made the tea, and I was given the once-over by her and her maiden Auntie Allie. They had never seen a foreigner before, let alone a Jewish one.

One morning, after an all-night session in my little hut, she arrived home with the milkman. As she let herself in, the screen door squeaked and her auntie yelled out, "Here she is, Maude. Here's the damned wretch. Your mother's been up all night in the gully looking for you."

Her mother refused to speak to her for a month, and she was forbidden ever to see me again. She was twenty-three; I said to her, "Listen, you're an adult woman. You can do whatever you want. I mean, you're not going to let your mother tell you that you can't see me." She said, "I could never lie to my mother. It's out of the question." But we did meet clandestinely. I'd pick her up from the office after work and we'd sneak off to a pub and have a few beers.

Later, I remember June admitting to me the moment she really fell in love with me. It was a Saturday afternoon, and I had taken her to a pub, a Melbourne pub, called the Riverside Inn. It was a lovely pub. I was wearing a double-breasted gray suit that I had brought with me from Singapore. She said she watched me go to the bar and fetch our drinks and bring them to the table where she was sitting. She said she watched my back as I was ordering the drinks at the bar and watched me coming back toward the table and fell in love with me, and I remember that.

There is a lake in the middle of Melbourne called the Albert Park Lake. It's an artificial lake, but I always liked it. It was a favorite place of ours to go parking at night. I remember it was a full moon and we were sitting in the car with the moon shining on the lake when I said to her, "What do you think about getting married?" I said, "I would like to marry you, but I'm not sure you should get married because you're a very good actress." We were both smart enough to know that if she got married the acting would suffer. Acting is the only thing she's ever been really serious about in her life. When she did eventually stop acting—in Paris, because of the language barrier—she was to go into a deep depression.

Then I said, "Why don't we live together? I don't mind getting married, but I warn you of one thing. My work will always come first. I will go wherever my work is, no matter how much I love you." Here I am, twenty-seven years old, and I know that already.

I also told her that we would never be rich. Maybe at some stage we would have enough money to have a nice apartment, but that seemed truly quite unreal in my head, because photography was so badly paid. So I advised her not to marry me, because I hate responsibilities. I thought that if I told her she wouldn't be able to say afterwards, "Oh, you talked me into it, you bastard." So I put it on the line, and she said, "OK, let's get married."

What was it about her? First of all, I'd never met an actress. Then she always made me laugh. She still does today. She was very amusing. She was a great singer too. I remember driving for hours in my "Veronica" with the side screens out and the breeze going and the sun shining, and June singing all these wonderful songs. Australian songs. English songs. Stuff from Shakespeare. It was a totally different affair from any I'd had with any other girl. Because all the other girls were really only about fucking. With her, there was another dimension.

I'd become very fond of June's mother. I remember sitting in her mother's bedroom, on the edge of her bed, with June. And I said, "Maudie, I would like to marry June, and June wants to marry me!" And she just threw up her hands and said, "What are you going to live on?" A very good question. And June said, "But he's got so much talent, he's going to be a great photographer." But her mother didn't understand anything about photography—the only photographers she knew were Athol Shmith, a very chic society photographer who later became our friend, and the street photographers that would stand on Swanston Street Bridge and snap your picture and hand out a card. So that's all she knew about photography. How could the poor woman know any more? So she said, "He's going to stand on the bridge. He's going to take street photographs of people. How are you going to live? What are you going to eat?" June said, "Helmut has this idea that he wants to get a car and travel through Australia with me, and through the Northern Territory, and just camp out to see the country." Well, that, of course, set her off. She said, "You'll die in the desert in the Northern Territory. You're going to die." You know, she was right, we probably would have.

So we sat in Maudie's bedroom with Maudie worrying about how we were going to survive. Anyway, June was very persuasive, because she really believed in what I was doing, which was quite extraordinary. I had exactly three pounds in the bank, which must have been worth less than twenty dollars in those days. She had nothing. Finally, Maudie gave her consent, but she insisted that we marry in a Catholic church. The place that was chosen was St. Patrick's Cathedral in Melbourne. The date was the 13th of May 1948.

I, being Jewish, had to have seven lessons from the priest in Catholicism; otherwise I couldn't be married in the Church. The priest was a very nice young man, who happened to be in charge of photography for the Catholic Church in the State of Victoria. I made it very clear to him at the beginning that I was not material for conversion to Catholicism and that, if we ever had children, I wasn't going to swear to him that they were going to be Catholic either. He was quite good about all that and realized I was a lost soul. We talked about photography. Eventually, we were married, although not on the high altar, because a Catholic cannot marry a nonbeliever on the high altar. They have a little altar on the side for terrible people like me. So that was that. Her sister got married two years later to a rich Methodist, and her mother didn't mind what fucking church they were married in. She was perfectly happy for Peggy to be married in a Methodist church, which June took very badly. It made me laugh; I thought it was very funny.

After the wedding, we went on a two-day honeymoon to Cowes, Phillip Island, before settling into our first bedsitter (which means a room with a bed and something to sit on). I remember the first time June cooked a meal. She'd

never cooked. She cooked sausages. I was standing next to her in the communal kitchen. It was outside the room on what they called the landing. Dreadful! It was dreadful! We shared the kitchen with a family called Maskell who lived in the room next to ours. They played the same record over and over again and sang along with it. "Rum and Coca-Cola." They played that fucking record day and night.

Once I knocked on their door and said, "Please stop it," and the guy came out. He was a big hunk of an Australian. I was never a great fighter, nor did I have any muscles. And he said, "I'll break ya fuckin' neck, ya bastard, I'll smash ya fuckin' head against the fuckin' wall." So I pulled my head in—in Australia you pull your head in—and went back to my room and shut the door. He was hot on my heels and tried to break it down, yelling, "Come out and fight, you bastard—come on—put 'em up!"

So, anyway, there's June cooking our first dinner of sausages. She put some butter or whatever you put in the pan, and I'm standing there watching her. I'm very proud of her. She throws the bangers in, and they spit because of the butter or the fat, and it goes all over her, on her dress or whatever she had on. So what does she do? She has a bad temper, and this Irish pigheadedness comes out. She takes the fucking frying pan and she throws the bangers on the floor and says, "Ah, fuck this." And I say, "You bloody well pick up those sausages and put them back in the frying pan—I want to have my dinner!"

The next fight we had was over Dora. On Saturday afternoons everyone in Melbourne goes to a beer garden. I had made a date with Dora to meet her for a couple of beers in the Faulkner Park Hotel. I don't know, I stayed maybe two or three hours, and I came home and June said, "Where have you been, Helmut?" I had had quite a lot to drink—the sun was shining on my head, and I was drinking all those beers. I was sort of yawning and tired. And I said, "I've been having a few beers with Dora." She went mad. . . . I can't remember what she said, but I remember that she was very mad that I had gone out with Dora on the first Saturday afternoon after our honeymoon and had these beers. So she threw a fit, and I said, "Listen, my darling, I'll just go for a walk, and when I come back, I hope that you have calmed down." And I just walked out, because I hate fights. I hadn't done anything— I was just having a beer with Dora. So I walked out and stayed away for two hours, and when I came back, she had calmed down. People generally do. And this is how I generally react to rows—I don't have rows, I just shut up. The next day, I've forgotten. I don't say anything, it's forgotten. I'm not the kind of guy that goes on and on.

To be able to eat and pay the rent, I did portraits and wedding pictures. I truly hated doing weddings. On Saturday afternoons, I would put up my camera outside a church, next to three or four other guys who were trying to snap the happy couple. One had to be watchful, because the guy next to you would surely try to open your dark slides and so fog all your film. You then handed out your card and hoped they would come by your studio to place an order.

June's job was to be the saleslady in the studio and to sell the wedding photographs to the brides and bridesmaids. They could choose black-and-white or sepia prints, hand coloring—which was more expensive—and miniatures in tiny gold frames that really increased the revenue because of the markups we got on them.

Unfortunately, June was the worst salesgirl you could ever wish for, and she hated doing it. I can still see her in the little office, sitting behind the desk, with the customer on the other side. She would pull out the samples of the frames, the enlargements, and the wedding albums, and she would try her best. She knew how much we depended on a sale. I'd open the door from time to time to see how she was doing. Was she selling? Was she doing well? And I was always terribly discouraged, because I knew she went through hell doing it. All the samples would be strewn all over the desk in front of the poor customer, and yet the orders were never as good as I'd hoped they would be.

One day June said, "If you hate it so much, why don't you ask for twenty-five pounds instead of ten pounds?" I said, "I don't know whether I'll get any-body at all at that price. We need the money, and ten pounds now is better than waiting for twenty-five." But she talked me into it, until I said, "All right, I'll give it a try." I put the price up by more than double, and I found that the people still came to have their portraits taken. That was very good.

I didn't have to do any more weddings. I was beyond that, and I was start-ing to do fashion pictures and catalogues, but the work was not good. How could it have been good? It was difficult to evolve as a photographer in Australia. Everything had to be a rehash of what was being done in America.

I got a regular job photographing the shop windows of a department store called Mantons. June used to come with me to help me at night when she wasn't playing. It was always cold when we did this—we had to stand in the freezing-cold wind that blew down Bourke Street. We took along a big black cloth that June held up behind me to keep the reflections off the windows. I used an old Thornton Picard camera that I had bought when I left the army for eight Australian pounds. It was made of mahogany and had a great big lens set in brass—a big plate camera from the 1930s. Three dark slides came with it. I would put up this old camera on a rickety old tripod and shoot away at all the windows. I would shoot six pictures, as the plate holders were double-sided. Then I would have to go back to the studio to reload, because I had no money to buy more plate holders.

No one lived in the city of Melbourne. They all lived in houses in the suburbs. Except for the cinemas and theaters and concerts in the Town Hall and a few Italian and Chinese restaurants, the city was deserted at night. I decided we'd live there.

I found a theatrical boarding house on Russell Street run by an English couple from the Midlands. I rented the only room that gave out onto the street, for a song. Breakfast was left at the door on a tray. The one bathroom was occupied at all hours of the day by an Aboriginal singer.

Because of the stifling heat in the summer, the window on the street had to be left open at night. One evening, after dinner, I was sitting up in bed reading the evening paper with June next to me when a drunk stuck his head in the window. He leaned on the sill and said, "Look at the fucking bastard, sitting up in bed reading the fucking *Herald*."

One of my clients made cabinets that looked like mahogany, with built-in gramophones and radios. He always ordered fifty prints of each model, and as there were about twenty different models this meant an order of a thousand prints at a time. I printed them at night on a homemade enlarger that was actually a converted studio camera turned upside down. The housing could not be moved, like that of a normal enlarger, so the table the paper was on had to go up and down instead. I was a terrible printer, but I couldn't afford to employ anyone. So I would expose the paper, and June would develop it in the developing dishes, fix it, and wash it.

She used to cook on a small gas ring in a little room that was used for drying negatives. All the hypo and developer would drip into the saucepan. (We had two saucepans—one for soup and one for coffee.) A rubber tube was attached to the gas outlet, and it leaked all the time. The developing of film was done in a small cubicle that we called Little Hell. The floor in the darkroom was made of an ancient tar malthoid. In the summer heat it would melt, and our shoes would get stuck in it. The temperatures in summer could reach 110 degrees Fahrenheit.

Advertising jobs were dished out in the pubs. One had to drink with the boys to get them. I didn't much like doing that. I always put my foot in it. Even today, I don't socialize much with the clients. The day came when the guy with the radio sets invited us to dinner with the wife. She was loaded before dinner, and became even drunker as the night wore on. She sensed my disgust and became abusive, and then she threw up all over me, and that was the end of my dream account.

Before I met June, I had only one client who had kept my head above water, and that was a mail-order catalogue called Rockmans, run by three brothers. It was distributed all over Australia, and they gave me all the work. I had to hand over half my earnings to the art director who had arranged the job. One bright day I was called into the office where the three brothers sat behind a desk. I stood in front of them like an idiot. They said, "Helmut, it has come to our attention that you are going to marry a shiksa." I didn't trust my ears. I said, "Well, yeah, I'm going to marry June. June Browne, yes." "Helmut, we don't understand. You're a good Jewish boy, and there are so many nice Jewish girls here. We don't think you should be marrying a shiksa." I said, "Well, it's got nothing to do with you." They said, "If you go ahead and marry this girl, you will never work for us again." I was living on this work, and there was a lot of it, but no one was going to tell me what to do. I've always hated being told what to do. I said, "Listen, I'll tell you what you can do." My latest pictures were lying on the desk ready to go to press. I picked them up and tore them to bits and threw them down in front of the brothers. I said, "I don't give a damn. I'm taking off, and you can shove it wherever you want to," and I stomped out of the office.

I was also warned by my friend Freddy Lewinsky not to marry a shiksa. One day, he said, she was bound to call me a dirty Jew or something like that. She never did, but I rant against Irish Catholics and call her all kinds of names.

I will not be told how to live or what to do, or how I should eat my soup. June says, "You can't go around burping all the time." I say, "I'll burp whenever I want, because it makes me feel better." I don't give a shit if I walk down the street and people turn around. I don't know these people. It may be a good thing and it may be a bad thing, my absolute resistance to conform to certain things.

My next source of income was from a magazine called *New Idea*, which still exists today. The work was dished out by a dear old duck called Miss Nethercote. She brought along knitted "layettes" of baby clothes—bonnets, booties, matinee jackets etc.—which I would arrange on a piece of paper and shoot from above, showing every stitch and all the detail, to go with the knitting instructions. She also brought knitted lampshades and sweaters, which June would model because I didn't have to pay her. June also modeled the

hats for a series called "Hat of the Week" for the bargain basement of the Myer Emporium, for the same reason. Poor June never got paid for her modeling work: I pocketed her money, reckoning I needed it more than she did.

At the end of the month, when the rent became due, a check or two would miraculously appear from these clients, the last but not least of which was Jeff Elliot, who was in charge of the Mutual Store food department. He would send around hampers of cheese and wine to be photographed—but not consumed.

At the end of the year, the clients would all call in for a Christmas drink and collect their presents.

June often used the little front office to entertain her actor friends. Sometimes I would come back from a job after lunch and wouldn't be able to get in the front door of the studio, because it was jam-packed with all her

actor and actress friends, who had not a sou, not a penny. June would be serv-
ing coffee and some cheap cake, and they would all be sitting around, laughing their heads off, drinking coffee, eating cake, and taking up space. I said,
"If we did have a customer, he wouldn't even have room to get into the bloody
studio." It was very funny. I adored all those people.

In the early 1950s, June toured Victoria with the Council of Adult
Education, which was supposed to bring culture to the locals out in the
boondocks of Victoria. The boondocks in Victoria are very large. Even
Melbourne in those days was not exactly a metropolis of culture. So June did
these tours for three months at a time, and I was left at home without her.

I used to visit her on weekends when they were not too far from Melbourne. And I would find a very closely knit company of actors and actresses who were living together day and night. They traveled from town to town in a thing they called the "monster," which held the actors up front, in the cabin, and the sets, the scenery, and the technicians in the back. They used to have a wonderful time getting drunk together and having parties. It was like a little army on the move.

The husbands and friends that came up from time to time for the weekend were confronted with a sort of united front against them. The troupe had inside jokes, they were bonded together, and it was like visiting a stranger. It was not very good for me, but, being the perfect person that I am, the angel, the perfect husband, I didn't make much of a fuss. It did create some kind of tension, though, and made me think, "Well, *she's* having fun. . . ."

I didn't think she was being unfaithful or anything. As far as I knew she wasn't. Anyway, that's her affair. I've never been a jealous person or a possessive person. I've always looked on jealousy as a sentiment that's nonproductive and totally useless. Even when I was a kid in love, if a girl wanted to leave, I always realized I could do nothing but let her go. There's a song that Marlene Dietrich sang that goes something like, "Why cry when two lovers part when on the next street corner there's already the next one?"

One day, June announced that she'd joined the Melbourne Repertory Company as a permanent member for a season, which meant rehearsing one play for two weeks during the day whilst playing another every night, with every second Sunday off. She didn't give a shit about me being on my own. I must say I was good enough to have never stopped her; in fact, during the weekends I used to "hold the book"—hear her lines.

We had a large circle of friends, and I used to take out some of the wives, especially on the weekend, when work slowed down. June was aware of this, but, Melbourne being the gossipy little town that it was, it wasn't long before "friends" began to call her and warn her of the "danger," even suggesting that

she quit the theater, which caused some marital tension. June kept right on working.

We had moved house a few times and ended up in a small comfortable flat in South Yarra. I was working on assignments for the Australian supplement of English *Vogue*, and in 1957 they offered me a twelve-month contract to work on *Vogue* in London.

So we flew off to Europe in a Super Constellation, a gorgeous four-propeller airplane with big leather seats and a ceiling of a midnight-blue sky

with stars. The trip, with a long stopover in Singapore, took two and a half days. Then we did the grand tour of Europe in our new white Porsche, which we collected in Stuttgart straight off the assembly line. Our daily allowance was one hundred francs, including hotels, food, and gas.

I have always wanted to retrace my steps. I've always been obsessed with going back and seeing the people I once knew. Strangely enough, as I get older the desire is leaving me. When June and I left Australia for London in 1957, we stopped off in Singapore and I contacted Josette. June already knew about her. I found her name and address in the telephone book; she had moved back into the same apartment in the Capitol Building. So I rang her, and then I went to see her on my own. At least I was smart enough not to take June along. It was like visiting the scene of your crimes. It was terrible.

The apartment was all black and dark—all the curtains were drawn—and she was half blind. "Ah," she said, taking the flowers from my hand, "sit, bébé." She could hardly see me, she looked terrible. When I saw her, Josette told me that Kitty had abandoned her and left for Australia alone with her family. Josette had been taken prisoner and had spent the whole of the war in the Changi prison camp.

She knew that I had always wanted to be a *Vogue* photographer, so I told her that at last my wish had come true and that I was on my way to England to work for English *Vogue*. I spent the afternoon with her, but I couldn't wait to get away. Although she was financially secure, she was a very sick lady. It should have taught me never ever to retrace my steps but I keep on doing it. That was the only really dreadful experience I've had.

CHAPTER SEVEN

LONDON *VOGUE* AND PARIS, *JARDIN DES MODES*, 1957–1959

I HAD NEVER BEEN to London, never been to England. The editor-in-chief of *Vogue* at that time was Audrey Withers, a lovely lady, very English—with a single-strand pearl necklace and twin set and everything that went with it.

The first day I arrived at the *Vogue* office was incredible. It was one thing working for *Vogue* in Australia, but it was another actually to land at the Holy Grail—the source. I said to myself, My God, at last, I'm a real *Vogue* photographer.

The euphoria didn't last long. The moment my first pictures came out of the lab, I knew I was in trouble. Depression set in fast.

We established ourselves in a horrible flat on Earl's Court Road. We had very little money. Although thirty pounds a week sounded like a lot, it didn't go very far. The flat was a four-flight walk-up and, together with Earl's Court Road, was the most depressing sight I'd ever seen. The studios in Golden Square were also depressing, and dusty, with terrible old wooden floors. I was told that under the grassy square in front of the building were the bodies of people who had died during the black plague. Somehow or other, it was indicative of my whole feeling for the place, my feelings toward working in

London. The whole area behind Piccadilly was depressing—Dickensian. In those dark days there was a lot of prostitution in the West End. In the tobacconists' windows were notices pinned by prostitutes that were mostly working out of little flats in Shepherd's Market. They advertised their specialties, such as "Strict English Education," "French Lessons Taught," and many more explicit handwritten advertisements, sometimes accompanied by a little sketch. What I liked best was "Strict English Education: Rod Will Not Be Spared," which seemed to sum up the English sex life.

A young photographer arrived from New York at the same time. He had been sent by Alex Liberman, art director at U.S. *Vogue*, to gain experience. His name was Claude Virgin, and we became friends. His photographs were sexy and different from anything that had been seen before in England. He became the favorite of all the fashion editors. He also had a unique way of photographing. He often worked with editor Unity Barnes, a proper schoolmarm who was very long and narrow. One day he went out to take fashion photographs of a model on Regent Street. This is how it was described to me by an assistant who was present at the sitting. Unity just stood there while Claude, his camera attached to his tripod, rubbed himself against it, timing his orgasm with the click of the shutter and crying, "Oh yes! Yes, yes, yes, yes, yes—that's it!" That kind of photography was quite unknown in 1957.

Claude's pictures were very, very good. I suffered from the fact that he was there, a rising star. My pictures were terrible and got steadily worse—more dreary, more boring, nothing like the pictures I had taken in Australia,

which were much better. The editors gave me a hard time. None offered help or advice.

I was an unsophisticated guy from the Australian bush who didn't know what to do. I didn't understand the English way of life—I wasn't interested in their way of life. I remember taking a photograph of a girl leaning against a lamppost and being told by one of the editors, "Helmut, a lady never leans against a lamppost." I didn't know where I was. I used to take my pictures home to June and she would just make a long face, the poor girl. She didn't want to depress me further. She said, "Oh, Helmut. Oh, Helmut. Oh, Helmut." I was totally confused, in a panic not to be performing the way I should have been. After my cushy life in Australia, where my ego had been fanned by my clients and my friends, and where I had no competition to speak of, I found myself out of my depth and struggling to stay afloat. The clothes I had to photograph were dreary and ladylike.

It was the year before the revolution on Carnaby Street and the start of the Swinging Sixties. Before Bailey, Duffy, and Donovan. It was twinsets and pearls and floral arrangements. There were two regular features. One was called "Shophound" and consisted of tiny little still-life photographs of scarves, shoes, and handbags. Then there was another, terrifying regular feature called "Mrs. Exeter." There was a sweet white-haired lady who was the regular Mrs. Exeter model and who modeled these clothes for the older woman. She must have been quite lovely thirty years before. So, while Claude got all the exciting model assignments, poor old Helmut from the sticks got "Mrs. Exeter" and "Shophound." If I was lucky I also got a couple of pages for yet another regular feature, called "More Taste Than Money." I was never given a top model to work with, like Susan Abrahams or Fiona Campbell Walters—not that I would have known what to do with them if I had been. The closest I got to the top was Enid Munich, and that didn't happen very often either. I put the poor girl through hell, once making her crawl around the studio floor eating grapes. God knows why I did that—it was a disaster!

The art director was John Parsons—a fey homosexual who could hardly bring himself to look at my contacts. I couldn't bear to look at him.

The star editor was Claire, Lady Rendlesham. She was as thin as a rake and as hard as nails, but she was the best. Her favorite photographer was Claude—she adored him. She gave me a really rough time. She treated me like some kind of peasant from the bush. She was right—I mean, I didn't show any promise or talent. She treated me with contempt, although a few years later, when I was on a roll in Paris, her attitude toward me changed entirely. She had left *Vogue* and had become the fashion editor of *Queen* magazine. At that point, I began to treat her terribly. I must say I can be pretty cruel, but when it's too easy to make someone suffer, I don't bother. June says, "Why do you let that person treat you like that?" And I say, "It's too easy to destroy them. When it's difficult to destroy somebody, it's more interesting."

During the collections, they would bring in famous photographers from Paris and New York to do the important collection pictures. Then not only I but Claude too would suffer pangs of envy and jealousy. I was so impressed with these guys. They would be flown in with their cameras and their assistants, and it was the most glamorous thing. All this helped to depress me even further, because I was very ambitious.

So there were these glamorous photographers flying in, and there were other star photographers—Cecil Beaton and Norman Parkinson and more. One day I was sent by UK *Vogue* to photograph Beaton in his country house. I took some snaps of him. Years later I was sitting waiting for Karl Lagerfeld in his apartment in Paris. I had started looking through a new book on Beaton when all of a sudden I saw in the credits "Frontispiece by Helmut Newton," and there it was—one of my snaps. I hadn't recognized it. It was backlit and very pretty, and it had nothing to do with me.

Many years later, in the 1970s, Beaton came over to Paris to photograph a collection for *Vogue*. I lugged my copies of all his books to the studio—three or four at a time—and I said, "Please, Maestro, sign these books for me," and he signed them to me. He had had a bad stroke and his writing was shaky, like a chicken's scratchings.

So, anyway, one day in London I decided I couldn't take it anymore. I had fallen in love with Paris on our grand tour of Europe. I remember the first time we stopped our car on the outskirts of Paris and had a cup of coffee on a café terrasse. I said to June, "You know, I have a feeling we're going to live here forever and ever—this is the place for us." But of course we continued on to London on our tour.

This illustrates how much I hated London during the time I was there: I lost my way daily en route from the flat in Earl's Court Road to the studio in Golden Square. I could never find my way. I have an inbuilt resistance to places that I don't like. In places I love, I am like a taxi driver. In Paris it took me a only few weeks to find my way around, and in Los Angeles I hardly ever stray, because I love the place. London was awful—I just suffered.

So, I decided, this was it. I said to June, "I'm going to break my contract. I'm going back to Paris, I don't care what they do. We'll take the Porsche and a couple of suitcases, and just go." June said, "You know, Helmut, you're taking an awful risk, because if you break your contract you'll never work for Condé Nast again." I said, "I don't give a shit, enough is enough." So, a month before my contract was up, I told Audrey Withers that I was leaving. She was actually most understanding. I think she was glad to get rid of me. So off we went to Paris, the Porsche loaded up to the gunnel with our few belongings.

At that time it was glamorous flying back and forth from Paris. There was an airline called Silver City owned by an Australian, and it took off from Le Touquet in France and landed at Lydd, on the southern coast of England. I would drive the Porsche into the front of the plane, and the cars were chained down—about five of them at a time—and then the owners and passengers would sit in the back of the plane on very basic seats. It took about twenty-five minutes or so to get across the Channel, and you could hear the cars bumping around against the bulkhead as we came in to land.

As soon as June and I arrived in Paris in 1957, we chose a hotel called Hôtel Boissy d'Anglas, a very old hotel on the rue Boissy d'Anglas, which runs parallel to the rue Royale and was a charming little street with wonderful little restaurants. We got the best room, the only room with a bath, for fifteen francs a night, including breakfast with café au lait, croissants, the works. The floor was at an angle, and when you got out of bed you had to sort of climb up a hill to get to the bathroom and the loo. Eventually, we found a flat in the sixteenth arrondissement, on the Avenue Mozart at the corner of the rue Jasmin.

We never had enough money to pay the rent and have a holiday. I remember saying to June one Easter, "What shall we do? Have a holiday or pay the rent?" and June said, "Let's have a holiday and not pay the rent." So we sneaked off in the middle of the night in our posh car and went to Switzerland, to a little place called St.-Cerque. We could only afford meat once a week and drank "Vin de Postillon" at one franc per liter.

I made the rounds of the Paris magazines with my portfolio and got a few offers and some knock-backs. One of them was from *Elle* magazine. There I was confronted by the all-powerful Peter Knapp, the art director, and at his side his star photographer, Foulie Elia. They looked at my portfolio and thanked me, and then, as I was walking down the corridor on my way out, I was followed by their hollow laughter. Many years later, Peter admitted that I was a pretty good technician.

In the end, I got an offer from *Jardin des Modes*. The art director at *Jardin des Modes* was Jacques Moutin. The editor-in-chief was a lady called Madame de la Viluchette, a woman I absolutely adored. At the time, *Jardin des Modes* was the most revolutionary fashion magazine in Europe. It had a fascinating history. Originally called *La Gazette du Bon Ton*, it had belonged to Condé Nast at one stage, had been bought and then sold by them. It was founded by a famous editor called Lucien Vogel. I didn't speak any French at all, and when people from the magazine rang me in the morning, I didn't understand what they were talking about. So I used to race into the offices, because I felt I could understand better when I was face-to-face with them. These were exciting days, when I learned all about fashion photography from those Parisians who really knew what it was all about.

Madame de la Viluchette was built like a battleship and had an imposing bosom and would dress in a rather old-fashioned way. She would sail through the editorial offices, and from time to time, when she came across me hovering in the shadows somewhere, waiting for an assignment, she would lift her finger and her head and look at me and say, "Newton, Newton, pensez à l'esprit de la mode—l'esprit de la mode surtout," and then I'd try to work out what that meant.

I learned everything from these Frenchwomen, the young ones and the old ones. The fashion editors were not only knowledgeable but also very good-looking. There was Peggy Roche—she looked like she was straight out of a French movie in her tight black skirt and her tight black rollneck sweater. She had a wonderful silhouette—she had what I thought was a great bosom—and beautiful legs. Then there was Souazique Calde, who later became editor-in-chief at *Elle*. I remember when she arrived as a young fashion editor at *Jardin des Modes*—we were all aflutter with the sex bomb that had arrived.

I remember the mornings when I got up early to go on assignments—I would go down and have a cup of coffee at the little café on the corner. There are a million little cafés at every corner in Paris. Let's say it's seven o'clock in the morning and it's summer and the clean water is running along the gutter. They have these funny little bits of carpet that make little dams to channel the water—this beautiful river runs down the gutter and down the street. It's all clean, it smells beautifully fresh, and the sun comes out—the light is gorgeous—and I stand by the bar and have a cup of coffee. The early workers come in and ask for "un petit blanc" and have their first little glass of white wine, and another "petit blanc" before they go off to work. They are blue-collar workers. Everybody mixes. Blue-collar workers mix with people going to the office, with girls.

It is elating, like being in a French movie. I had never wanted to be in an English movie.

As a photographer, it was good for me to see this life. I lived in a universe that I adored. Even the noise of the traffic, even the look of the cars, even the buses—the buses had a platform at the back of them. The smell of Gitanes cigarettes. Every little particle of Paris life was a joy. I learned about fashion from the French—how they are born with it, the way they dress.

As I have said before, I have always been very interested in prostitution, since I saw Red Erna at the age of seven. There is something about buying a woman that excites me. One of the things that used to excite me was the concept that the woman was like merchandise—that you could walk along a street with two hundred or three hundred prostitutes of which 150 were extremely desirable-looking in the middle of the day with all the traffic going by.

The rue St.-Denis was the street of the whores and little hotels. Every door, every café, every little bar was full of whores. The street is very,

very long, and the whores and hotels are on both sides of the street. It's not like a red-light district—normal life goes on. People live in little apartment houses, they are not all hotels. A woman goes out shopping with her kid, passes one hundred whores—that's just the way it is, and nobody worries about it. It was a mixture of normal everyday life with a kind of sinfulness.

The way the whores dressed was extraordinary. Even they had an inborn feel for fashion that was brought out in the way they dressed themselves to attract the customers—a sense of showing what their specialties were by the way they were dressed.

I remember well one that I was struck with was dressed in a white wedding dress with a veil. Many were dressed in boots—really high boots, like military boots—with whips, and chains around their necks and around their arms. Then there were some who dressed very chic. There were a lot of old whores that did very good business—women of fifty, really used-up-looking women. In fact, they did a very good trade. A lot of men seemed to prefer going to these women, because they were like their wives or their mothers or something. At times I went with one or two of the women, because it was very interesting to me. I saw the interior of the rooms, which were extremely poor and rickety and tiny, with funny old bedspreads with flowers on them.

These were not bordellos. These were hotels. The customer chose his merchandise and paid for his room. The girl got a towel from the concierge, who took the money for the room. Everything cost very little in those days. I don't know what the prices are now—I haven't been.

Although there were cops around, the cops were around more to protect the girls than the customers. You were not allowed to take photographs—it didn't say "Don't Photograph," but I remember trying to and learning that if you did you would get beaten up, so I quickly packed up my camera. It was better to have been stopped by the cops than by the girls, who would sure as hell have beaten me up if I'd persisted. This was because many of the girls came from the country, and they did not want their families to know what they were doing.

When we had visitors from abroad, we used to take them to dinner and put them in the car and show them the sights of Paris. June thinks it is extraordinary that I never confessed to her how often I walked alone there. It was a world that I was totally attracted to. So these walks were very frequent but very private.

There was also a wonderful bordello in Berlin, on the Knesebeckstrasse, which runs parallel to the Schluterstrasse. It was in one of those typically enormous Berlin apartments that have long, long corridors with at least ten rooms and a very large living room, almost like a ballroom.

I remember discovering this bordello and going up there by myself. In the large living room there was a bar and you could have a drink—you didn't have to go with a girl if you didn't feel like it, though the girls were wonderful, good-looking, and in various stages of dress or undress. Nobody did a hard sell, it was very civilized. You had a drink and then you chose one of the girls, and if you were happy with the kind of services supplied, you would go back and ask for the same girl again. Of course, sometimes one would have to wait quite a long time, because she was busy with another customer.

I've taken a lot of photographs in Hollywood of girls in water-bed motels along the Ventura Boulevard with the TV sets showing porno movies—very weird. They're entirely different from what it was like in Paris.

In 1957, I also worked for a magazine in Berlin, called *Constanze*, to make enough money to keep on living in Paris. It wasn't the first time I had been back. Before June and I had left Australia, I had bought June Christopher Isherwood's *Goodbye to Berlin*. We had stayed in a pension similar to the one described in the book, and had a wonderful time on the town—nightclubs, bars, restaurants, cafés. I had revisited all the places of my childhood and the lower depths of Berlin then.

I remember my visits to bars, cabarets, and Kneipen where I took many photographs during my frequent trips to that city. There was Chez Nous, a wild homosexual bar with a marvelous floor show. There was a "Kim Novak," the spitting image of the real thing, who sang and danced and as a finale whipped off her bra and wig to reveal a beautiful blond German boy; there was a sultry Marlene Dietrich, complete with top hat and tails, about 1.90 meters tall, with a deep throaty voice; and others. I used to sit at the bar, have a few drinks, soak up the real sinful Berlin atmosphere, and talk to these guys in between acts. One day I took June there; she was horrified to see me on such good terms with these people.

They worked us very hard at *Constanze*. We were only let out of the studio in the evenings—it was like living in a kind of school. The magazine owned the whole top floor of a building off the Kurfürstendamm. The studio in this building was an old sculptor's studio, and all the models and photographers had little rooms and slept on the premises. We had to pay a very nominal sum for rent, like fifteen Deutschemarks a night, and we got lunch and breakfast thrown in. It was pretty terrible.

We were never let out of the studio until we had finished our quota of I don't know how many dresses, and there always seemed to be more and more hanging in the studio, on racks and racks. It was servitude. Once we had finished our work for the day, we were allowed out to have a good time in Berlin.

Why didn't I do advertising? Not only did I not know how to go about finding it, but I had understood at a very early stage that you had to become an editorial-magazine photographer in order to become an important fashion photographer. I was not going to become famous doing ads, but if I stuck to editorial photography my pictures would be credited to me, and I knew this was the key to eventual success.

This is where June was a tower of strength. She didn't say, "Go out and earn more money so we can buy meat." She understood perfectly my desire, my ambition to become a great fashion photographer. Anyway, as I've said, when one chooses photography, one does not choose it to make a lot of money.

I rejected studio work. I was very unhappy in the studio, although when we did the "haute-couture" collections we weren't allowed to take the dresses out into the streets or parks. This was before television. It was only TV that broke the taboo established by the Chambre Syndicale in Paris against taking the models of the new haute-couture collections out in public. The Chambre was obsessed by fear that the Paris creations would be copied by the cheap manufacturers. And with good reason.

I used to wrap the girls up in white bedsheets and drag them over into the Jardins des Tuileries, where I, in a very circumspect and clandestine manner, would photograph the haute-couture models. Life was wonderful, but I wasn't making enough money to make ends meet.

IN THE 1960S, I developed a severe case of overactive thyroid that caused terrible attacks of fury in public. I got thinner and thinner. Friends laid bets on how long I had to live. I was shaking like a leaf. People thought I was on drugs. Doctors were sure I had cancer. One day, Susan Train, the Paris editor of American *Vogue*, sent me to see Dr. Jean Dax, who diagnosed me immediately and cured me in less than six months. Jean became a friend and was to come to my rescue at another moment of my life, as was Susan Train.

Early in 1959, I bought two tickets back to Australia, on the day when June was asked to go back to London for six months to play Nurse Jane, the same part she'd played in a BBC radio serial called *The Flying Doctor* during our year in London. So we packed our bags, and she went to London and I flew back to Melbourne.

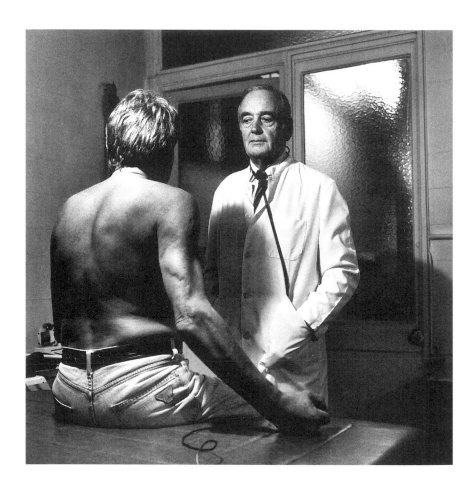

CHAPTER EIGHT

AUSTRALIAN *VOGUE*,
1959–1961

BOUGHT THIS really pretty house in East Melbourne, with a pretty front garden and big backyard. It was an old Victorian house. I hadn't told June anything. She was playing in London, so it was a surprise. After six months, the radio serial finished and she was on her way home.

In those days they flew a big four-engine airplane called Britannia from London to Melbourne. It was a notoriously bad plane that broke down not once but three times from England to Australia, and one never knew when it would arrive. It was the biggest plane flying at that time.

June was supposed to arrive in the evening of a certain day of the week, and I had thrown a party with all her friends and a lot of beer and grog. This was a surprise—she thought we were still living in our little apartment in South Yarra. The plane was late; it was late by five hours, then it was late by twelve hours. But the party went on, in true Australian fashion. We just got more beer and more liquor in, and I kept on ringing the airport. Everyone was getting drunker and drunker. . . .

At last they said the plane was arriving, so I took my car and drove out to the airport and picked her up. I said to her, "There's a party going on; all our friends are waiting for you there."

She was tired, having been so long on this dreadful plane. And she said, all of a sudden, "But that's not the way home." "No," I said, "the party is at a friend's place." She was too dead to question that. So I drove her to the new house. And as everyone was saying "Hello, hello," I said, "You like the house, June?" And she said, "It's OK, I guess." I said, "It's yours."

And she burst into tears—she just hated the idea. First of all, she hated coming back, hated leaving England, which she loved. She didn't want to come back to Australia. She made me promise to take her back to Europe in two years, when I had made some money.

The party ended on a very bad note, as far as I can remember. The next morning, she locked herself in the house, and for weeks she did not go out. She was so unhappy. She hated the house, she felt it was a stone around her neck, but I had bought this house with the last penny I had, and it was a lovely house. Her friends used to knock on the window and scream, "June, we know you're in there; open the bloody door, open the door!" She wouldn't. She'd just lock herself in and not answer the door to anybody. It was a terrible period.

Then she got into this TV company that was like a repertory company, and she loved it. They were doing regular plays once every two weeks or once a month. It was live television, which was very unbelievable. The plays were live, and there was no recording of any of them.

I remember her walking in the door one night after she'd played Hecate in *Macbeth*. "Who was that sexy girl playing Hecate?" I asked. I hadn't recog-

nized her. She was also a wild and wonderful Hedda Gabler. Playing live drama on television must have been the happiest time of her life.

The next crisis came when I said, "Two years are up, we're going to go back to Paris." She said, "I don't want to go." I said, "I'm going." Australia was not a country where a photographer could make a great career. You can only make a great career in fashion photography in Paris or New York. You can't go anywhere else.

By then I had a big studio on Bourke Street with my friend and partner Henry Talbot, and we now had ten people working for us. We were doing well. I had a contract with Australian *Vogue* that gave me good standing, even though most of the pictures were dreadful. When I told our accountant that I was chucking it all, he said, "Helmut, in two years you will have two beau-

tiful cars in your garage, a boat in the bay. Your financial future is assured—
don't do this."

I replied, "Fuck this, I want to be a famous photographer." And I said to
Henry, "Give me two thousand dollars and two cameras, and you keep the
rest."

Then a letter arrived from Alex Liberman, the director of U.S. *Vogue*,
telling me in no uncertain terms to stay in Australia. The company needed me
there. There would be no work for me at English or American *Vogue*.

It was 1961. We rented out the house and left for Paris again.

Once more, someone had tried to tell me what to do, so I did the opposite.

CHAPTER NINE

FRENCH *VOGUE*, 1961–1983

ND THEN I got my big break. I joined French *Vogue* and my career
took off. For twenty-three years, I did my best work for French
Vogue. I also went back and forth to London for English *Vogue*, which
had changed for the better after the invasion of the East End photographers
and the cultural revolution.

By now, no one was going to fuck me around anymore. I knew just what
kind of photographs I wanted to take. And they knew, if they asked me, that
they were going to get something pretty sexy. No more "Mrs. Exeter" for me.

Alex Liberman sent a memo to Italian *Vogue* warning the editor-in-chief
to beware of the erotic content in my pictures. The editor-in-chief of English
Vogue was then Beatrix Miller. She called me "Shifty Newton," because her
friends would look at the magazine and say, "How could you publish pictures
like that? They're indecent." I was slipping them in wherever I could. They
were pretty mild by today's standards. They didn't all get through.

I also worked for *Queen* magazine, which was a truly revolutionary and
fantastic magazine. It was owned by just one man, Jocelyn Stevens. The art director was Willie Landells, who became one of my best friends. The fashion
editor with whom I worked a lot was Claire, Lady Rendlesham, who, after

my bitter experiences on English *Vogue* when I first worked in London, became another friend.

My work began to make a small impact on the people in the business, which shows the power of editorial work and credits. If you did great ads and your name was not on them, who was going to know? Who was going to care? They lacked the prestige and impact that editorial work had. One of the great things about French *Vogue* was that, although we were very poorly paid (150–200 francs per page), we were left totally to our own devices. The 1960s and '70s was a most creative time for fashion photography. We didn't need money to produce our photographs.

IN THE SUMMER of 1964, Courrèges presented a collection that created a furor. I was working with Claire Rendlesham on the haute-couture collections for *Queen* magazine. Claire, who was a great journalist, decided to ignore all the other houses and only report on Courrèges. It was a scoop and a sensation.

It was, of course, understood, as far as I was concerned, that I would never divulge any work I did for French *Vogue* to another magazine, and vice versa. When all the magazines came out with the story of the haute-couture collections for that season, Françoise de Langlade, the editor-in-chief of French *Vogue*, called me into her office. She was furious, really furious. She had *Queen* on her desk, and she slapped it down and said, "Helmut, what is all this about?" I said, "Well, you know, although I work for French *Vogue* I'm not under contract." So she said, "But you should have told me what you were doing, what you were up to." I said, "No, of course not. I wouldn't discuss any of the work I do for you and French *Vogue* with anybody else, and I would not dream of divulging any ideas that have been developed by another magazine." We had a tremendous row, and I was thrown out and for two years found refuge with *Elle* magazine, where Claude Brouet, a great fashion editor, was ruling the roost, and we became close friends.

Two years later, when Françoise de Langlade left for New York, Francine Crescent became editor-in-chief and invited me back to French *Vogue*. I didn't need much persuasion, and from that moment on, through the early 1980s, I stayed with French *Vogue*.

The 1960s was an important moneymaking period for all photographers. It was a very rich period, with a lot of work around, and the prices began to get interesting.

I took a mortgage on the house in Australia and bought an apartment in the oldest part of Paris, called the Marais: a wonderfully romantic, historic part of Paris, peopled by clochards, drunks, and whores. Our French friends thought we were crazy to spend money on such a neighborhood. But we loved it. (Soon after we moved in, the city of Paris classified the whole district and it became fashionable.)

When June's mother came from Australia to visit us for the first time, in 1963, the apartment wasn't even furnished. Friends were sleeping on the floor on mattresses. Maudie arrived at Le Bourget, and we picked her up from the airport. As we drove into our part of town, she looked at the narrow, grimy streets and buildings which to us were very picturesque and tried to hide her shock. She said, "Is this where you live, Junie? Is this where you live, Helmie—ahhhhhhhhh!" You could hear she didn't want to say, "My God, what a terrible neighborhood! What has happened to them?"

We lived and worked in that apartment on the rue Aubriot for fourteen years, until the construction of the Pompidou Center, when the traffic on the rue de Rivoli became impossible and made prisoners of the people living in the Marais. The metro was the only way out—this was before the tunnels were built.

The year after I bought the apartment on the rue Aubriot, we bought a stone ruin with a small vineyard in Ramatuelle—fifteen kilometers from St.-Tropez. The vineyard produced about ten thousand liters of wine every year. We spent all our holidays there: Christmas and Easter, all of June, and half of July. On July 14 we moved back to Paris, because from then until

September 1, it was deserted. There was an enormous exodus. Everything closed down. You could park your car anywhere. The people who spent August in Paris were called "Aoûtiens"—Augustians. Then, on September 1 we would drive down south again in our Bentley.

It was early in 1964 that I decided I had to own a Bentley. I went to Franco-Britannic, the Rolls-Royce and Bentley dealers in Paris, and walked with the salesman through the basement garage, where the secondhand motorcars were displayed. I told the guy I had ten thousand francs to spend, and he showed me a number of clapped-out "R" types. In the corner of the garage I saw a silver-and-blue metallized beauty. I said, "That's the one I want." He looked at me pityingly and said, "Monsieur, you don't have enough money for that one. It's Madame Peugeot's car in which she goes golfing. The price is twenty-three thousand francs." (In those days the French still counted in "old Francs," so one had to add two more zeros.) About a month later, on a

Saturday morning, there arrived a check in the mail from the advertising agency Scholz and Partners. I had done a job for them, and the check was for the exact sum needed to buy that car. I hotfooted it to Neuilly, gave the salesman that check, and said, "Give me the car, quick." He looked at me like I was crazy, but I had the car and drove it home in a state of complete euphoria.

JUNE FOUND the adjustment to living in Paris difficult as far as her work was concerned. Her acting days were over. She could not afford to go back and forth to London anymore to pursue her career. Nobody was going to call her and pay her trip over. It was too complicated. We had a good time with friends, but she was unhappy doing nothing. She hated just being Mrs. Newton. Then, one Christmas, I gave her a box of paints and some canvasses and she began to paint and became a painter—she was pretty good, not bad at all. She gave some away but there are still some left.

Then, in 1970, she became a photographer. She had always worked with me very closely and was interested in photography, but had never thought of taking up a camera herself. One day I was sick in bed with the flu and I had a job to do for Gitanes. The client was in London, so nobody would have been any the wiser as to who photographed the model boy, who was waiting on the Place Vendôme. As someone had to keep the appointment with him, she said she'd go, and offered to take some pictures of him at the same time, knowing that if she failed I could reshoot the following week. So I showed her how to use the exposure meter and how to load the camera, and off she went and did it. The client never queried it, and it ran in an English advertising campaign. She was pretty proud, and that's how she became a photographer.

June had a lot of lucky breaks, and she has a fantastic eye. She became a very successful photographer, with museum shows, books, and catalogues, but she never really had the energy and the single-mindedness as a photographer that she had had as an actress.

O UR FAVORITE restaurant in Paris was the Brasserie Lipp, which is still going strong today and is still frequented by movie and theater people, politicians, poets, opera singers, and lovers. Sunday lunch was a who's who of who had slept with whom on Saturday night.

The late Mr. Cazes presided over his temple with a rod of iron. Holding his little book and pen at the ready, he would look at you over his glasses very seriously, and unless you were Mr. Pompidou or somebody very important, or else a nightly regular, he would say, "Three hours' wait, or upstairs in one hour," and you'd put your tail between your legs and slip away. Nobody wanted to be upstairs.

The more known I became, the less time I had to wait for a table. First it was three hours, then it was two, and then one. One of the bonuses of notoriety seems to be the ease with which one can get a table in almost every city in the world. Now, when I go to Paris, all I have to do is call and say, "Helmut Newton here," but sometimes I still have to wait.

Another favorite restaurant was La Coupole, especially during the collections, when it was packed with American clients and buyers. There one waited for a table in the American Bar. The maître d' was a Berliner, so I got fairly good treatment. Opposite La Coupole is a bar for night owls called Le Sélect, where we downed Calvados and beer chasers after dinner at La Coupole.

When the film *Blow-Up* came out, the Bar du Théâtre on the Avenue Montaigne was the place to be. It was crammed with photographers and models during the collections. You knew who was out of work by who was in the Bar du Théâtre in the evening. It was for sure that the guys that were working were not in the bar—they were in the studios. This bar was jammed with young men who walked around with six Nikons around their necks even though they were not working. The young people, everybody, wanted to be a fashion photographer. It became a big cult.

Opposite Fouquet's, on the Avenue George V, there was a bar called Alexanders. We used to hang out there with our friends Jacques and Patty Faure. She was a photographer, and he was the art director of French *Vogue* and *Adam*. After dinner or the movies or both, we'd end up at Alexanders for a nightcap or two, then go on to Harry's Bar for hot dogs and beer. All four of us smoked as if there was no tomorrow. We gossiped like mad, talked about projects, the latest books, some written by authors we were proud to know, and collections. We missed them terribly when they moved to California, where a few years later Jacques died. Patty remained with their daughter, Zazu, and became the successful owner of the Patricia Faure Art Gallery.

S HORTLY AFTER the Berlin Wall was built, Jacques asked me to go to Berlin for French *Vogue* to do a photo *roman*, which is like a little movie in photographs. I told the story of a beautiful Russian spy. The model was Brigitte Schilling. It started with her photographing documents, etc., etc., and it ended up with her being arrested by two Berlin cops. In the series there's a photograph of Brigitte standing on one of the towers that looked over the Wall.

Unfortunately, in all my enthusiasm for getting the Berlin ambience and the spy ambience into my photographs, I didn't notice that, at the foot of the observation tower by the Wall, there was a plaque and a cross for the first guy that had come over the Wall from the East and been shot by the Eastern border guards. When the story came out in the magazine, it created an international political scandal. The German newspapers were full of it. They were enraged by the fact that a fashion magazine was, as they saw it, making fun of a serious thing like the Wall. They were outraged by the whole thing. The reaction of the German fashion advertisers toward French *Vogue* was that they canceled all their advertising contracts. It was a huge debacle. The then editor-in-chief, Edmond Charles Roux, was very elegant about it and never, ever blamed me.

I had wanted the story to end with my spy being decorated by a Russian general. I had told June about the development of this photo *roman*. In the middle of the night, during the shoot, June had telephoned me in my Berlin hotel from Paris and said: "Whatever you do, Helmut, the West must win." Just as well she said that, because things would have gone from bad to worse had the Russian spy been the heroine of this piece.

Another thing that was very sad was that Brigitte Schilling, who at the time was a very big star model in Germany and all over Europe, never got another job in Germany, because she was associated with my photographs and nobody ever forgave her. Also, the two cops that posed in my pictures were fired from the force. It was about two years before the whole thing blew over and I could set foot in Berlin again. All my Berlin friends dubbed me the "Mauer [Wall] Helmut."

EIN FOTOGRAF „VERKAUFT" BERLINER MODELLE

Mode an der Mauer

Mannequin auf Abwegen: „Mata Hari 63" — Räuberpistole auf Hochglanz

VOGUE
EUROPE

PRÉSENTE

MATA·HARI
VERSION 1963

avec

BRIGITTE SHILLING
Dans le rôle de Mata-Hari

TOURNÉE

en extérieurs dans les ruines de Berlin
en intérieurs à l'Hôtel Hilton, Berlin

GANTS de Guibert Frères
CHAUSSURES de Ch. Diop-Roger Vivier

La garde-robe de Mata-Hari est de Uli Rich-
ter, Gehringer & Glupp, Schwichtenberg,
Veitsch, Lauer-Böhlendorff, Detlev Albers, H.
W. Claussen,Staebe-Seger, Heinz Oestergaard,
Studio Dress, Lindenstaed & Breitschneider.

PHOTOGRAPHIÉ ET DIRIGÉ PAR

HELMUT NEWTON

● Mode-Fotografen bevorzugen Kontraste: Ätherische Mannequins vor
Männern mit dem Preßlufthammer, zarte Modelle vor Düsenjägern,
verwegene Creationen in zerfallenen Villen ... Um die Modelle der
Berliner Haute Couture vorzustellen, brauchte die Pariser Ausgabe der
berühmten Modezeitschrift „Vogue" nicht lange zu suchen. Fotograf
Helmut Newton strickte eine Räuberpistole an der Mauer: „Doppel-
agentin Mata Hari 63". Hier ein paar Proben aus diesem Modebericht:

„Es geschah im Januar 1963 vor der
Berliner Mauer, in der Nähe der Char-
lottenstraße ... Wie kann man sehen,
was auf der anderen Seite geschieht —
und wie die verbotene Zone inkognito
durchdringen?

Unsere Mata Hari steigt auf eine der
Aufpasser-Plattformen und greift zum
Opernglas. Der Umstände wegen be-

müht sie sich, ihr Gesicht unter einem
Hut in der Farbe des Himmels und mit
hängender Krempe zu verbergen ...
Lange Handschuhe, um Fingerabdrücke
zu vermeiden. Das Ensemble ist diskret
und zieht nicht die Aufmerksamkeit
auf sich ...'

So beginnt die Geschichte, die das
Mannequin Brigitte Schilling sodann
in denkbar abenteuerliche Situationen
— und immer neue Creationen, ver-
setzt.

„Mata Hari' empfängt einen Ge-
heimauftrag, klettert durch Ruinen,
spioniert mit dem Teleobjektiv, ent-
rieht ein Verzeichnis, klaut Doku-
mente, fotografiert mit der Minox,
speist bei Aben, lernt zunächst den
„Mann mit dem Monokel' und später
den „Mann mit der Nelke' kennen —
und kommt schließlich in den Besitz
einer Aktentasche, die sie ,von einer
Zone zur anderen' zu transportieren
hat ...'

„Ein Wagen hat sie bis an die
Grenze begleitet. Sie hat nicht mehr
als eine Viertelstunde, um den Marsch
durch die neblige Nacht und das
feuchte Gras zu machen. Aber plötz-
lich ... War der „Mann mit der Nelke'
ein Verräter? Aus einem Jeep springen
zwei Polizisten. Die Aktentasche wird
ihr entrissen. Mata Hari wird festge-
nommen. Wohin wird man sie führen?

Mit dieser bangen Frage beschließt
„Vogue" seinen Bericht.

Der Leser ist aber nicht nur froh,
daß die Agentin noch geschnappt
wurde, sondern kommt auch zu dem
Schluß:

Recht geschieht ihr, wenn sie zu
ihren strapaziösen Unter-
ocht eine praktische und
lltagshält, sondern im-
Xtravagante Modelle zu

VORGEFÜHRT — UND AB
wird „Mata Hari 63" verhaftet
sie Gala: eine spektakulär

DER IDEALE ANZUG für Besuche an der Mauer? Irrtum — mit diesem Foto
eröffnet die Modezeitschrift „Vogue" eine Bildergeschichte von unfreiwilliger
Komik: „Mata Hari 63" (alias Brigitte Schilling) präsentiert Berliner Modelle.

Modeling Clothes At Berlin Wall Held 'Tasteless'

By the Associated Press

BERLIN, Feb. 11.—A magazine
report about Berlin fashions displayed at the Communist wall di-
viding this city was strongly criticized today.

Heinz Mohr, president of the
Federation of Berlin's Ladies Garment Industries, called the report
"tasteless."

The report appears in the Feb-
ruary issue of "Vogue Europe," a
fashion magazine printed in Paris.

Mr. Mohr found "especially tasteless" a photo of a model displaying
a white top coat, white hat and
black skirt while standing on a
wooden podium which West Berlin
police have set up to allow to see
over the wall.

Another picture shows a model
in an evening dress being led away
from Communist barbed-wire fences
by two rain-coated West Berlin
policemen.

Many of the dresses shown came
from Berlin's leading fashion
houses.

Mr. Mohr's statement complained
that neither he nor the federation
had been consulted beforehand
about the magazine article.

"It must be feared that our already difficult situation in Berlin
will be further complicated by the
article," Mr. Mohr said.

AUTO-PHOTO...
Keulbachstraße 82-86
Besonders günstige Finanzierung

Berlin über Mode-Photos an der Mauer entrüstet

Berlin (AZ) — Mit Empörung
hat die Berliner Öffentlichkeit
am Montag auf eine Veröffentlichung der Pariser Modezeitschrift
„Vogue-Europe" reagiert, in der
das Münchner Starmannequin und
Photomodell Brigitte Schilling in
neuen Kleidern und Abendroben
an der Berliner Mauer als „Mata
Hari 1963" abgebildet worden war.
Heinz Mohr, der Vorsitzende der
B-rliner Damenoberbekleidungs-
industrie (DOB) erklärte in einer
Stellungnahme, er sei „außer-
ordentlich schockiert" über diese
siebenseitige Veröffentlichung in
der Zeitschrift. Als „besonders
geschmacklos" bezeichnete Mohr
ein Photo, das das Mannequin an
einem Polizeibeobachtungsstand
an der Sektorengrenze des Berliner Bezirks Kreuzberg zeigt —
unweit der Stelle, an der im
Herbst 1962 der Ostberliner Bau-
arbeiter Peter Fechter starb.

Italiener

URING THE SIXTIES, French *Vogue* founded a new supplement attached to the haute-couture collection number. It was called "250 Models" or "300 Models," which meant three hundred dresses. We called it the "tracassant," which meant a "worry," or a damn nuisance. All *Vogue* photographers were told: "You work on the tracassant or else no more big pages in the real *Vogue*." This is the way the tracassant worked: each photographer was set up with an assistant, a truck, and a driver and was sent from one couture house to another. We had our lights and "polecats," which are stands from which you hang a white seamless background, and we would start at eight each evening and work through the night, photographing dozens and dozens of dresses until the early morning. In each house we would set up the background and our lights, trying to make it look good, although this was practically impossible. There were mobs of little pictures on the pages. Sometimes you got a full page, but not very often, and yet there was nothing we could do, because we wanted to get our big pages in the magazine for the rest of the year. It was the most awful kind of slavery—it was blackmail. But it didn't last long. The idea was given up after a few years.

Not only did we do the tracassant during the night, but also more creative work was done for *Vogue* proper. I used to sit up with June for nights and nights on end thinking of wonderful ideas for the pages in *Vogue*. I would shake the ideas out of her until she came up with something I could get my teeth into. We would smoke packs and packs of cigarettes without filters, devour bottles of Scotch, sitting until the early hours of the morning and thinking of ideas. June would say, "What about this?" and I'd say, "No, no, you can do better than that!" It was rather nerve-racking, but it was also very exciting.

It was June's idea to do a scene from Hitchcock's film *North by Northwest*— of the airplane chasing the girl. She gave it to me on the telephone and I just said, "Ah, it's a great idea." It was very difficult indeed, but I did it. In order for the plane to be in the picture, the pilot had to fly low. It was up to me to direct him so he could make the lowest approach possible, to be in my frame.

He warned me that he could only make a right-hand turn at the end of the field. In the excitement I gave him the wrong signal. When he landed he was furious—he had followed my instructions and practically crashed. He showed me the grass on the wing tip of his plane.

The magazine photographers were outdoing each other everywhere, producing entertaining and amusing fashion photographs that were not just showing the dress, but were well beyond that. The town was absolutely jam-packed with photographers who had great ideas.

I remember strange coincidences that made us realize that ideas, even if kept secret, seemed to float around like telepathy between New York and Paris. At one stage I was doing everything with mirrors, and I can't remember who, but somebody else came from New York and did everything with mirrors, and then mirrors were in every damn magazine.

It was an extraordinary, euphoric time. I realized that certain countries and their women inspired me more than others. France, Germany, and America became my major stimuli. And the most beautiful women in the world were coming to Paris, because they were the ones that were wearing the clothes. And then there were the house models, a very different breed from the photographic models. They showed first of all to the press, then to the buyers, and then the public. The great couture houses had "cabines," big dressing rooms, where the house models in white overalls sat all day waiting to be called into the salons. The shows went on for many, many weeks. When the professionals had seen everything, the houses were opened to the tourists. Tickets were difficult to get—people queued up and begged to be let in. So these house models had employment for many weeks. They earned very little money, but they had class.

Some of them had what was called a "protector"—a rich gentleman who was always married and would pay the girl's rent, in exchange for which he would visit her once or twice a week. She would possibly still have a boyfriend on the side, but she also had this middle-aged man—generally a good bourgeois, a lawyer, an industrialist, something like that. An excellent, practical, and very French arrangement.

I have a friend who is in his early forties and all he dreams of is to be the protector of a girl like that, but these models don't exist anymore, and nobody's going to give sexual favors to somebody who just pays the rent—those days are just gone forever, like the wonderful Paris custom of "Cinq à Sept," which meant leaving your office at 5 p.m. and having a gallant rendezvous until 7 p.m., when Monsieur would return home to wife and family for apéritifs and dinner. A perfect French arrangement ruined by the impossible Paris traffic at that hour.

Now there are star models who get a fortune for every show, and everything is on video. The big show is videoed, and the people come to the salons and buy from the video, so it has become very uninteresting. I cannot describe the mystique of those days of the Paris collections.

The shows took place in the fashion houses, and in the summer the heat from the spotlights was unbearable. Everyone was crammed together, sitting on those classic little gilt chairs. The first row was reserved for the great editors—from *Vogue* and *Harper's Bazaar*—the Americans were the most important people—and also the editors-in-chief of the big French magazines with their assistants, who sat in the row behind them. The hierarchy was strict.

The most important magazine photographers were given the most important couturiers' creations; the lesser talent was given something less important.

So you'd arrive at the studio at around 7 p.m., supervise the model's makeup, talk about the hair. The hair was actually dictated by the fashion designers. They would say: "For this collection, I will have this hairdresser, who will do one hairstyle that will follow right through the collection." So, in a way, we had to adhere to the hairstyles that were done for each designer. Later on, years later, the whole thing became looser. It's changed so much that now you can do anything you want.

So we would be sitting around, drinking coffee, talking to the models, and smoking a million cigarettes, because the dresses hadn't arrived. The dresses never arrived. Because every magazine wanted the same dress. The more important the magazine you worked for, the quicker you got the dresses.

We used to work until five or six in the morning. It was the usual thing, and it went on for a week. And I remember coming home and June saying, "How can you do it? You must be dead!" and I'd say, "I am dead!" But as soon as I got up, I went to the studio to look at my contacts with the editors, and the battles began.

Invariably, I was unhappy with their choices. Today things are different, and have been so for many years. I just submit a very small choice of photographs to the magazine I'm working for.

During the mid-seventies, French *Vogue* was under the rule of Robert Caillé, Director of Paris Condé Nast. Caillé, in many ways, was a terrific president. He gave us total editorial freedom, as long as the photo sittings did not cost any money. I used to say that the magazine let us photographers loose in the streets of Paris like wild dogs to bring back the most outrageous pictures that only French *Vogue* would ever have the courage to publish. It became the mecca of daring and we were the envy of every foreign photographer. To get anything out of Robert Caillé, he had to be approached well before lunchtime; his canteen was Maxim's and the lunches were long and highly alcoholic. We were told that a half bottle of Scotch was the daily ration; of course, none of us were ever invited to share food and drink. So the late afternoons in the office, after these lunches, were never very fruitful or constructive.

Around 1975 came an edict from Robert's office: all photographers' negatives had to be surrendered to *Vogue* to be kept in its archives on the Place du Palais Bourbon. That period was especially important to my work. It probably was when I did some of my best pictures. So, I got busy with scissors and started cutting up my rolls of film, surrendering what I felt I had to, to keep "them" quiet, and saving the best negatives for myself. Poor Robert died in 1981 in the aftermath of the Maxim's lunches. We missed him badly, but under the direction of Francine Crescent, the *Vogue* went on to break all the rules and remain the most exciting fashion magazine in the business.

Years later, a woman who had the job as archivist of French *Vogue* decided that all this was just too much trouble and threw all the negatives into the trash can outside the door of No. 4 Place du Palais Bourbon. Soon after, I received a notice from British *Vogue* informing me that all my contacts and negatives in the London office would be destroyed by a certain date, unless I came to London to collect them. June took the next plane to London and returned triumphantly with most of the stuff.

During the '70s I had started to contribute more and more to a new English magazine called *Nova*. It was the most innovative publication and my work there was totally different from my French *Vogue* pictures. It was stimulating to see my work in all these different publications. Italian *Vogue* and *Amica*, French *Réalité*, *Stern*, *Paris Match*. I valued the creativity of many of the fashion editors I worked with during that period: Polly Mellen, Grace Coddington, Franceline Prat, Manuela Pavesi, Caroline Baker. Later it was women like Phyllis Posnick and Anna Dello Russo who contributed their talents to my work.

And yet, how times have changed: before the '80s none of the editorial people would have been caught dead speaking to anybody in the advertising department. The art director and the editor-in-chief decided what would be printed in the pages of the magazine. They were all-powerful. The guys from the advertising department were like traveling salesmen and were called "space salesmen." Nowadays they are elevated to the title of "Publisher" and they have usurped total power. But luckily there still are some interesting editors-in-chief, Anna Wintour in New York and Franca Sozzani in Milan. They could not be more different in their editorial policies, but much of their choices are dictated by the more liberal mores of Europe and the very strict confines of the religious right and the tastes of Middle America. Sometimes Anna lets me get away with a wild story, but often my pictures are heavily censored.

In the late '90s a Christie's auction catalogue landed on my desk. Among other offerings, it contained a collection of fashion photographs from French *Vogue* and the provenance was "Collection of Jocelyn Kargère." Kargère had been art director of French *Vogue* for a number of years and had regularly raided the drawers of the art department that held the prints returned from the printers. At that time I happened to be in London, and

Christie's asked me to view these prints. I did, and the sale was immediately canceled.

All photographers have many sad stories like these to tell, our prints, stolen or not returned, turn up at auctions in reputable houses, on Internet websites like eBay, and we are powerless to stop this practice. Years ago I hit on an idea: all prints at magazines or with clients that were not returned would be billed out at an outrageous price—$4,500 each— whatever their size. These prints carry no identification, such as stamps or signatures, except for an archival number.

· · ·

AMERICAN STORES bought from the couturiers in order to copy the designs and make cheaper clothes. They paid a lot of money for that, and that's why the French hated the piracy, which started with people sketching during the collection; they lost a lot of revenue. It was difficult to police, but when someone was caught sketching, he or she was thrown out of the house. The exposure of the shows on TV broke all that up.

We had our friends amongst the photographers. I had a great friendship with a young German photographer called Chris von Wangenheim that started during a Rome collection. I met him in the bar of the Hotel Inghilterra, where all the photographers were staying, and from then on we became very close friends. We had both been born in Germany, and he recognized what other people see as a very Germanic, very Berlin, influence in my pictures. He also saw the success this had brought to me. He tried to emulate my style and was very influenced by my work, especially the sado-masochistic side. I was much older than he was. My work has big echoes in his work. We had a lot of fun together; he was a wonderful guy and a great photographer. He was killed in a tragic car accident in 1981.

I've never been given a grant by an institution, and I've never been given a scholarship, but I've always known how to use the resources of my clients—either advertising or editorial. I called it "beating the system." What I did was to set aside one hour or maybe two hours of the sitting for my own uses. Naturally I let them see the photographs, but these were generally of such a nature that they preferred to publish the straight versions rather than the private versions. In this way, over many years I built up my personal archives. Not only did I have the use of models, makeup artists, and hairdressers, I also had the use of fashion accessories, or whatever else there was at the sitting.

CHAPTER TEN

NEW YORK,
MRS. VREELAND, AND
ALEX LIBERMAN, 1965–1973

IN 1962, Diana Vreeland, always referred to as Mrs. Vreeland, left *Harper's Bazaar* and became editor-in-chief at American *Vogue*.

In 1965, she phoned me in Paris and said: "Mr. Newton, I would like you to come to New York, bring a beautiful girl with you, and work for the magazine." This was a fantastic opportunity for an ambitious, still-unknown photographer. It meant lots of money and, if I was successful, a tremendous boost in my career.

Little did I know that this was never going to work for me, and that my pictures were going to be miserable and unmemorable. Mrs. Vreeland's vision was one of fantasia, Moroccan extravaganzas, rouged heels—yes!—and dreams of exotica. Mine was of a highly sexual woman, in all respects Western, whose native habitat was Paris, Milan, and maybe New York.

But I tried and tried. I spent miserable days in the New York studios trying to satisfy Mrs. Vreeland's every wish. I was invited back to New York the next year, only to experience the same disaster. But I was still trying. So important were New York and American *Vogue* in the career of any fashion photographer that I was blinded by dreams of fame and money. It was an expensive and hard lesson for me. The third year, Mrs. Vreeland asked me to photograph the Paris-collection leading pages for the magazine, which was a great honor. She sent a telex to Paris: "Mr. Newton, we want you to do the Spring collections in New York. They will be green and white and I want you to refer back to the pictures that Mr. Avedon took here last year for the black and white issue." At last I woke up from my American dream and replied, "Thank you, but I'd rather not."

Mrs. Vreeland's working routine was extravagant and most unusual. She would make her grand entrance into the office at noon after her masseur had massaged her at home, where Mrs. Vreeland had checked photographers' contacts from the previous day's sittings. From there would come the very imperious judgment as to whether they had to be taken again or if they were OK. In most cases the judgment was "Retake!" Never have I worked on a magazine that spent so much money on retakes. It was quite common to have five to eight retakes, not only for me but for many photographers who were working for the magazine. Many times people would be sent back on trips abroad, Morocco, anywhere; money was no object.

Completely confused by Mrs. Vreeland's extravagant desires and banned from going into my beloved streets, I was told to work only in the studio. I ran up and down Third Avenue, sweat dripping off me, peering into those awful antiques shops, looking for props to satisfy Mrs. Vreeland's taste for the exotic. Needless to say, my photos looked just awful.

The result that Mrs. Vreeland was looking for was the only thing that counted, that mattered. The fact that she didn't come in until noon made the fashion editors' jobs slavery. I remember passing her office, the famous office decorated in red lacquer, with leopard-skin-covered chairs and couch. Her door was closed, and outside there were chairs and benches where the fashion editors waited to be called in, to be told what to do and what not to do, to be given her imperious judgment. What was terrifying was that it was any time between six and ten o'clock in the evening when I saw those fashion editors sitting and waiting to be called in. I realized those poor women didn't have any kind of private life. The fact that everything was telescoped into the time between three o'clock and the very late afternoon or evening made it very hard for everybody.

Another great event was Mrs. Vreeland's descent on Paris for the haute-couture collections. *Vogue* owns a beautiful building on the Place du Palais Bourbon in Paris, which was always ready to receive her and all her secretaries. This was not good enough. Mrs. Vreeland took over the second floor of the Hotel Crillon—just about every room in there. She installed her own switchboard and her own secretaries. It was a most extravagant way to run a magazine.

Early in 1971, Mrs. Vreeland was fired from *Vogue* in a sudden, ignominious, and dramatic manner.

Late in 1971, the phone rang in my apartment in Paris. It was Alex Liberman on the other side of the Atlantic. He said, "Helmut, I want you to come to New York and do forty-five pages for American *Vogue* in the same spirit as you have been working for French *Vogue* for the last nine years." I had never heard him say this kind of thing before, because what I did for French *Vogue* had always been anathema to American *Vogue*.

Alexander Liberman was the nearest thing to God at *Vogue*. Elegant and always dressed the same way. Married to a wild Russian, Tatiana, who was one of the scariest women I ever met. Years later, after she died, Alex confessed to me that he too was very scared of her. As creative director, he ruled *Vogue* and us photographers with a rod of iron. We knew, if he called us into his office and called us "Friend," we were in deep shit.

As always, I learned a lot from Alex. In 1972 he sent me to the island of Maui in Hawaii to photograph swimsuits. It never stopped raining. In a panic I rang Alex in New York and bleated over the phone, "I can't take my pictures, the weather is terrible." To which he replied coldly, "Helmut, I am not interested in the weather, I am only interested in the pictures you will bring back."

That was a lesson I was never to forget. You got to bring back the bacon, that's why they send you into the field.

But he gave the magazine the great style that it lost when he left. When he retired, the spirit of the magazine without him died slowly. He lived in Miami, and I always went to see him on my yearly visits there and for the first time, after all these years, we became close friends. He had an uncanny feeling of what would come next. He encouraged his photographers to produce fashion photos that looked like snapshots and then, later, would publish some of my riskier images against the wishes of editors and publishers. He was the first to recognize the genius of Larry Flynt and quoted him, "Show the pink." At his departure he made sure that his successors would never be able to fill his shoes.

And so I thought that his offer was a golden opportunity to do the kind of work that was right up my alley for American *Vogue*. I left Paris in November 1971 and went to New York.

I HAD BEEN burning the candle at both ends in Europe over the last six or seven years, because my work had involved four collections a year for French *Vogue* and then four collections in Milan and Rome. At that time I was a freelance. I had no contract with Condé Nast, and I was allowed to do what I wanted and take on as much work as I could fit in, which was a lot in those days. The collections were photographed at night, so they could be shown to the buyers during the day. When I was in Rome we'd never, ever go to bed. I remember well that during the summer of 1971 I spent seven days in Rome photographing, and at the end of the week my assistant said, "Do you realize, Helmut, in seven days we have slept twenty hours?"

It really was a kind of self-inflicted wound, this urge to try to become the best. I was smoking heavily and drinking quite a lot. I was not smoking anything as silly as a filter cigarette—we were smoking Lucky Strike and Camels, the real stuff.

We used to have a great time with all the models. In the summer of 1971, my assistant in Rome was a French vicomte. Probably the best assistant, apart from Fifi, I've ever had—an ex–racing driver, very small and very good-looking, an absolute charmer.

That was the time when I was really trying to make the maximum amount of money. There was so much work, and every photographer who worked reasonably well in those days made a lot of money. I made a lot of trips all over Europe and North Africa. On those trips, wherever we were, the team generally consisted of fashion editors, hairdressers, and models. In the morning, when everybody came down for breakfast, all the women used to be smiling broadly, happy as larks, because the vicomte had run from room to room and just about fucked everybody that wanted it, and kept the whole female crew extremely happy. He was an excellent assistant, an absolute delight to be with.

So, in that late autumn of 1971, I arrived in New York completely worn out after all the work I had done in Europe. I was run-down, short of breath, and my heart was banging away, but I didn't take any notice of this, I just started work for Alex. It was very hard going physically. It was also very cold, which was bad for me, I think. All the work was criticized, because at times I overstepped the mark for American sensibilities. Pressure was put on me not to go too far in my European way of photographing. But I did some nice pictures, and I recall at the time that I was fascinated by the Art Deco architecture of New York, exterior and interior. I took many many photographs of the old Twentieth Century Fox offices, which are beautiful. I scouted around the Chrysler Building; the lifts were just marvels of design, and the building material was wonderful. The Indian heads, the wood paneling in the lifts, the heavy metal doors, everything was a kind of architectural wonderland for me. I worked day and night.

Then there was a public holiday and I got very, very sick. It was a Friday evening—it always is, that kind of thing always happens on a public holiday. I went as an outpatient to a hospital near my hotel. I waited for hours, and they took one look at me and said, "We don't know what's the matter with you, you seem OK to us," and sent me away. There was no doctor around, because everyone was out of town for the holiday.

On Monday I went on with my work for *Vogue* magazine. By now it was quite late in the year. We generally traveled around New York in a big location van and a limousine, because I never worked in the studio. We were out in the streets one afternoon, working at Fifth Avenue and 69th Street. I was working near the location van, and I had the girl somewhere in the road, to get the traffic in the background, when I seemed to faint. I remember holding my camera up in my right hand. I fell onto the roadside, and people who witnessed it told me my arm was straight up in the air to save my camera as I went down. I got myself back up. People were a bit worried, but I said: "No, I'm OK, I'm OK." We continued taking photographs, and then the same thing happened again, except this time I couldn't get up.

People from the team helped me up. We were parked right outside a doctor's office, and the editor, Gloria Moncur, immediately took me in and said: "Quick, quick, get the doctor!" We went into his office; the doctor took one look at me and said to her, "Get him out of here immediately and into Lenox Hill Hospital."

Again I was lucky, because it was only a few blocks away. I was lucky to be so near to a good hospital which specialized in heart diseases, and also in having a limousine to take me there.

As they rushed me to the hospital, I realized that I couldn't speak. The strangest noises were coming from my mouth. It was quite horrible for me to listen to, so I stopped trying to talk. They delivered me into the emergency ward, and I was on a bed. The doctor came and asked me questions about where I came from, my age, and so on, and I couldn't reply, because this horrible sound was coming out of my mouth. Then he gave me a pen and said: "Write the answers to my questions on the bedsheet." So I tried to write and realized that I had no power to hold the pen—I was unable to write, with either my right or my left hand—I was a total vegetable. I could understand

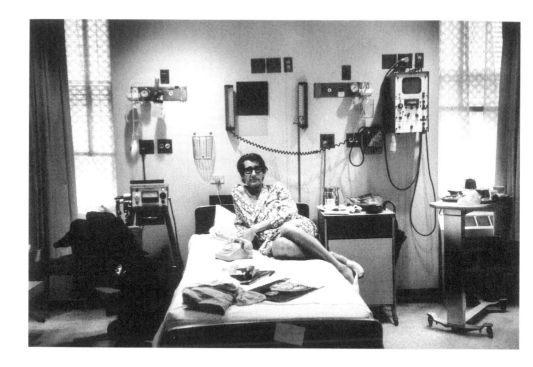

everything, I knew exactly what was going on around me, but I couldn't communicate anything to anybody in any possible way.

It was the scariest moment in my life. I lay back on the hospital bed in
front of all the doctors and just gave up. I just didn't make any effort. I was
resigned. I didn't seem particularly worried, I had no pain or anything, but I
had a terrible fear of not being able to communicate.

Within three hours, by some miracle, I had my power of speech and
strength back. This was like manna from heaven for me, it was incredible.
Then I thought I was perfectly all right, which of course was not the case. It
appeared that a blood clot had shot off from my heart, onto my brain, and my
heart was unnaturally enlarged as a result of the crazy life that I was leading—
the work I'd been doing, the worrying about it, the longing to be the best
fashion photographer, maybe in the world. Ever since I had started I had been
extremely ambitious. I wanted to do beautiful work. I wanted to be the best.

There I was at the Lenox Hill Hospital, on I think a Thursday night. I had just about finished my forty-five pages. The doctors had worked extremely fast; the people were just fantastic. There was one young doctor who was the first to look after me when I started to find my speech and gain all my powers back. He said: "We're going to do a lumbar puncture." I remember that June, who seems to know a lot about medical matters (it always astounds me that she knows where all the insides of a person are, when I have absolutely no idea), had said: "The worst thing that can happen to anybody is a lumbar puncture." So I said to this young doctor: "Oh Jesus Christ, a lumbar puncture, that's supposed to be terribly painful," and he said, "Not if you know what you're doing." He turned me around on my stomach, and before I could say "knife," he had given me the injection. I didn't feel anything—there was much less sensation than at the dentist. Afterwards, he said: "Well, you've got to know exactly what spot to hit."

In the middle of the night, the chief doctor came around and he said: "I'm going to ring your wife immediately, she must come at once to New York." Of course, at that time I had no idea that I was passing near the "critical point." I only found out much, much later that the following three days were to decide whether I would live or die. The doctors were concerned that more than one blood clot would shoot off from my tremendously enlarged heart.

I was given a particular exercise to do with my thumb and my middle finger. Apparently this tells you when something's coming on, when you lose feeling in it or something like that. The moment I felt something in the tips of my thumb and middle finger, I had to ring the emergency bell by my bedside. So, throughout the night, I did this, I kept on feeling myself whenever I woke up. The doctor asked for my telephone number in Paris and rang there and said: "Mrs. Newton, you must come immediately to New York to come and be near your husband." I said to the doctor, "Could I please speak with her?" and he handed me the telephone. I said: "Hi, darling, I'm very much better! I don't think there's any need for you to come, and anyway you have no American visa." I knew that June was terribly vague about this kind of thing, like renewing passports or visas or anything like that. She would arrive somewhere in New York, at the airport, and they wouldn't let her in. But the doctor grabbed the telephone again and he said: "Mrs. Newton, I am absolutely definite, you must get on the next plane to New York and be with your husband." He also told June that I had had a very heavy stroke.

June later told me that she had rung Susan Train at the American *Vogue* office in Paris, and that Susan had moved heaven and earth to get her a visa over the weekend. They opened the consulate on Saturday morning, thanks to Susan's efforts, and June was on the plane on Saturday evening. She arrived on Sunday morning and was at my bedside and stayed. When she had to go to sleep she went back to my room in the Blackstone Hotel, which was forty blocks away. She had to come by bus every day.

When she wasn't there right on the dot for visiting hours, I used to do my nut and say, "Where the hell is she?" and "What's she doing?" I think she had become friendly with some woman who also visited her husband, and I think they went out for coffee or something. Happy hour, no doubt, happy hour round the corner from the hospital.

I'm a very egotistical person. I always think of myself first in every situation. When June arrived from Paris, the doctor brought her in and said, "Here's your most precious possession." I said, "Ha! *This* is my most precious possession." And I pointed to myself. It came from the heart. June has never forgotten that.

Everybody from the magazine was absolutely fantastic. Grace Mirabella, the editor-in-chief of American *Vogue*, came, and I was my usual horrible self. I said: "It's all because of you and those forty-five pages!" June said I was horrible, but she knows what I'm like, anyway. Grace forgave me. She came very often. Mr. Irving Penn offered to do the last, missing pages for me, but Alex thought June might like to do them. June thought it was a lovely idea. So she finished this enormous article that ran over two or three months in American *Vogue*.

At that time I was friends with Elsa Peretti, who visited me daily, always

bringing me amusing presents. She was a stunning beauty, tall, with one of those wonderfully raspy Italian voices, willful and capricious, and a great designer of jewelry for Tiffany's. I photographed her often, dressed as a *Playboy* Bunny and nude. Being a good friend, I didn't bother to get a release to publish her photos. She allowed me to publish the Bunny portrait but said, "For the nudes, Helmut, you have to wait for the death of my father." Well, he died a long time ago. Anyway, this was a lesson to me to insist on a release, even from my very best friends.

The company paid the hospital bill. Mr. Newhouse, the owner of Condé Nast, is terribly chic, very elegant about everything. If you have to work for a magazine corporation, I don't think anybody can do better than to work for Condé Nast. They really are the most generous and caring people in many ways.

I was so keen to get out of the damn hospital, and to take up what I thought would be a normal life again, that whenever the weekend came (of course all the doctors stopped work and left New York for the weekend) I used to lie in my hospital bed and say to June and to anybody else around, "What are the fuckers doing?" and "Why aren't they working on me? I don't want to lie here on the weekend, I want them to get me right. I want to get out of here as soon as possible. They are paid enough money to work over-time. Let the fuckers work over the weekend. . . ."

After two weeks in hospital, they let me out for Christmas. We shacked up in the Volney Hotel, a few blocks from the hospital. I will never forget how June and I walked through the cold, freezing streets of New York, in

beautiful sunshine. I was very, very cold, all wrapped up. I dared not go by myself. Then, one day, I plucked up my courage and, leaning on June's arm, I said, "Look, you just stand on this street corner and let me try to cross the street by myself." That was another experience that I don't think I'll ever forget.

One day I rang Grace Mirabella and I said: "Listen, Grace, I know I'm shaky"—"shaky" was putting it mildly, I could barely stand on my feet, I was as weak as a kitten—"but you know I would like to try to take some pictures in my hotel suite." Two models were hired—Margaret Ramme and Vivienne Fauney—and *Vogue* sent along some lingerie. I could barely pick up my little 35mm camera, but I had an assistant and my five-hundred-watt photo flood, and I started taking pictures. It took me a long time. I think it took me about half a day to do one photograph, and then I had a rest, and then I did another half a day. But it was a series of lingerie photographs that was very successful for American *Vogue*.

In January 1972, I had to go back to Lenox Hill Hospital for a catheterization of my heart. That's when I met Simon Stertzer, the doctor who was to do the catheterization. From that day on we were friends.

When they wheeled me out of the operating room after the catheterization, I was clutching my little automatic Minolta. Two nurses wheeled me past June, who was sitting in the corridor waiting, and she overheard one nurse saying to the other, "What the hell has he got in his hand?" "A camera." "What's he going to do with it?" "He thinks he's going to photograph himself."

Everything went fine, but I became a fibrillator, which meant that my heart rhythm was totally irregular, and I was told not to exert myself, because my physical output would be cut by about 50 percent. This was depressing news. My first question was, "Can I still work as a photographer?"

They said, "Yes, you can, but you must remember that you are a fibrillator, that you will never have the output of a normal person, you will have to look after yourself and be careful."

In 1973, June and I went to Australia to see her mother, who was celebrating her eightieth birthday at that time. June went ahead and I went via New York, because Stertzer had decided that he was going to give me electric-shock treatment to shock my heart back to a normal rhythm. When the electric-shock treatment was finished, Simon Stertzer said I had spoken French right through the treatment and swore terribly but never said a word in English, just kept on speaking French and swearing. Anyway, by the time I got out of that treatment, my heart was back to a normal rhythm. I cannot tell you the difference that made to me. I rang June and said: "Listen to my heart. Can you hear it? I'm not a fibrillator anymore." We were both ecstatically excited. I was a different person. With this new heartbeat of mine, I set out to join June in Australia. I remember sort of sprinting along the airport to catch my plane in New York with a feeling of great exhilaration to be able to experience this physical output, which I hadn't had since 1971.

One Sunday afternoon, two weeks after I arrived in Melbourne, I was sitting in the kitchen of June's mother's house when I felt my heartbeat go back into fibrillation. It was tremendously depressing. It just didn't work, for a couple of reasons. When I rang Simon Stertzer in New York, he said that it was better to go back to being a fibrillator, rather than have another shot at the electric-shock treatment. They put me on medication without first testing its reaction, and it produced severe diarrhea. There were other medical options, but it was too late to try them.

The first thing I did when I returned to Paris after my heart attack and stroke was to sell my beloved Bentley. I was never satisfied with the service of the Paris Bentley people and instead would drive regularly to Geneva to keep my beauty in perfect condition, fly back to Paris while she was being serviced, fly back to Geneva to collect her, and drive back to Paris. Too much waste of time. All I wanted to do was simplify my life and take pictures. Instead of driving to our house in Ramatuelle, we would fly.

I've always found that work is my best therapy. Everything seems to cure itself when I'm working. Physically I feel better. My little automatic camera that I had with me in the hospital helped me to forget. The camera in the suite

at the Volney Hotel and the series of lingerie photographs helped me a good way along the road to recovery. There is something about a camera. I find it can act as a barrier between me and reality.

Another thing that marked the 1970s for me was the publishing of my first book, *White Women*. It was very important at this stage in my career, because a book gives a photographer an authority that magazines and newspapers can never offer. There were two people instrumental in pushing me to make the book. One was June, as always a moving force behind my work. She always made me start new venues, try out new things. The other person was Xavier Moreau, who had become my agent. June met him while I was absent from Paris on a trip, and she liked him and we became friends.

Bea Feitler designed the book, and June was its editor. June thought up the wonderful title, although once she had thought of it she got scared and

said, "You, a Jew, can't possibly have this kind of racist title on your first book," and I said, "Bullshit, it has nothing to do with being racist, this is a great title. What's more, there isn't a black girl in this book." There were, however, about ten men in it, and a couple of them sent me a telegram saying, "I'm proud to be a white woman." The book made a big furor because it was the first of its kind. The term "porno chic" was coined in connection with it.

In 1977 I fell in love with an apartment on the rue de L'Abbé de L'Epée the moment that I saw it. June had already seen it while I was away in New York but hadn't mentioned it to me. I bought it in five minutes, and it almost broke up our marriage. June hated that apartment, but I loved it. She especially hated the bathroom walls, which were lined with Portuguese marble, so she had the marble ripped out. We'd been told that the previous owner had committed suicide by throwing herself from the salon window. We later found out that she'd blown her brains out in the bathroom. June said, "There you are, I felt all along the vibes were bad in this apartment." I said, "I don't feel any vibes and I don't give a shit how many people kill themselves, I'm not going to kill myself—to me this is the most wondrous place." I called it my dream palace and made it beautiful, and we lived and worked in it until we left Paris for Monte Carlo in 1981.

CHAPTER ELEVEN

MONTE CARLO,
1981–1982

ITURNED SIXTY-ONE at the end of 1981. I had been living in Paris for more than twenty years. I loved it. I loved working for French *Vogue*, photographing the city, every street corner, the most secretive parks, the outer suburbs called "La Zone," and creating this character I called the "woman of the 16ᵗʰ Arrondissement" with too much money, wearing wonderful clothes by Yves Saint Laurent, Dior, and . . . But now I felt I needed a change from the ever-present tax examiner, who extracted 70 percent in income taxes, not to mention all the other, indirect taxes that we in France were burdened with, plus the weather that over the years seemed to get grayer and rainier and colder than ever. And I can't stand the cold and gray skies. So we decided to move to Monte Carlo, where the sun was shining and you lived tax-free. I consulted a lawyer, a specialist on Monaco affairs and residency proceedings.

Our bags were packed for our annual departure to Los Angeles at the end of December when the lawyer guy rings me and says, "Mr. Newton, if you are serious about going to live in Monte Carlo, don't leave for Los Angeles, go to

Monte Carlo now, and try and get your papers." So June throws everything out of the cases and repacks for the south of France, and we leave for Monte Carlo. We shack up in the Hermitage and go and see Mr. Courtin, chief of the Police Department, who decides on the fate of residency applicants like us. After questioning us on our intentions for our future life in the principality, he looks at both of us kindly but sternly and says, "Come back here in eight days." Which we did, and there were our residency permits.

Then June got sick. A major operation was absolutely necessary. And so the worst year in my life started. It was January 1982. We went back to Paris. June had made a date with the surgeon in the hospital to perform the operation. Then she caught a cold, which meant that she could not be operated on, she couldn't have anesthetic, and everything had to be put off. She was terribly worried, and it is very hard for me to describe the anxiety that I experienced. You know I never think of anybody else but myself. I didn't think about her—no, I did indeed, I did of course think about her, I worried about her like mad—but I was also worrying about myself. I was thinking, "Oh my God, what am I going to do without her, if anything happens?"

We made a number of trips from Paris to Monte Carlo. We had found an apartment we liked. Our dear Dr. Dax said to June, "While the going is good, before your operation, you'd better keep busy and establish your household as soon as you can. There's nothing you can do until you get into the hospital." So we remained in limbo, traveling between Paris and Monaco, worrying, trying to move the household goods from Paris and from Ramatuelle. It was the strangest period of my life. I seemed to be totally ineffectual in this crisis, and June proved to be a rock of courage and strength.

In the end, she was operated on in April 1982, and of course I took photographs. As I mentioned earlier, I find the camera can act as a barrier between me and reality. When I have to face something that is very unpleasant, like my heart attack, and my slow recovery in the hospital in New York in 1971, taking pictures from my hospital bed helped a lot. And when June underwent this enormous operation in 1982, I could face her and I could face

the things that they had done to her body much more readily and much more courageously when I had my camera between June and my eyes. It's always been like that. I've always thought that a war photographer wouldn't be able to face the bloodshed and the war if he didn't have his camera between him and the horrors that he was recording.

The camera was a wall between me and the pain of others that I couldn't bear. The pain of June that I couldn't bear. The operation was successful. She was extremely weak, I mean weak like I'd never seen her weak before. The professor who had done the operation called me into his office and said, "Now, listen, Mr. Newton, your wife is extremely weak, and at no time must she have any psychological upset. She must be absolutely tranquil; you must help her as much as possible. You have to be extremely nice to her, loving toward her, and she must not be worried about anything, because the slightest worry is going to aggravate her postoperative condition and could prove extremely dangerous to her."

What did egotistical, weak little Helmut do? Well, of course, he let the side down. He did exactly the opposite and had a complete collapse in Monte Carlo.

A week or so after the operation, we moved into our apartment in Monte Carlo. June was very weak and had a lot of problems. I had to help her out of bed, I had to help her into the bathtub, I had to help her on the loo. She was physically very, very weak. But as always, she was very strong mentally. I also helped her into the swimming pool of the building. She swam gently back and forth with me guiding her.

I took to the streets of Monte Carlo and walked around all by myself. I remember I was so depressed, I felt as if I had never been as depressed in all my life. There was the wrench from my Paris life; there was June's illness and helplessness; there was the fact that, for the first time in my life, I did not live in a big city. I had been born in a big city and I had always lived in a big city. All of a sudden, I was in a strange place called Monte Carlo, and it was not a town, not a watering place, not a resort. Monte Carlo is a very special place and there's no other place quite like it in the world. In a way it reminded me of Singapore in the colonial days, but smaller, much smaller.

While June had her rests, I would take the bus and go to the gardens known as "Little Africa," near the Casino, and sit on a park bench and start to cry.

I had not brought my car from Paris; I had sold it. I had not taken the jeep from St.-Tropez; it was still at my house in Ramatuelle. I didn't want to drive, as I thought I would certainly crash; I had no powers of concentration. I was never going to pick up a camera again. When I was in the apartment, I followed June around like a dog. She was my tower of strength. Instead of me being the strong one and keeping everything away from her, she carried the load on her shoulders. How she did it, I'll never know, because all I remember is that my depression got worse and worse. When I went out to do the shopping I would play Russian roulette with the big trucks, the cement trucks, the construction trucks, the gravel trucks that carried stuff to the construction sites, which are numerous in Monte Carlo.

They used to barrel around the roundabout in front of our building at high speed. In order to do my shopping, I had to cross numerous streets to get to St.-Roman, which was the nearest shopping center, in the street that I call La Rue Sans Joie, "The Street Without Joy." Even in Paris, even if you live in the best or richest neighborhood, somewhere in sight there is always a Rue Sans Joie. We had the same looking out of our window in the Luxembourg in our last apartment, and I photographed that joyless street many, many times. Well, this joyless street at the back of our apartment building in Monte Carlo was one of the most joyless streets I'd ever seen. Of course, now, after twenty years, I have become used to it, and, of course, I am not depressed anymore. Now I just love Monte Carlo and my life here.

But back to the spring of 1982. I became so depressed that I rang my friend Dr. Jean Dax. Jean has always been there for me whenever I have needed him—to get me over a cold, to make me able to go back to work. Jean was always there, the witch-doctor who always seemed to have something to get me back on my feet throughout all those years. Anyway, I told Jean that I was very sad, and I told him what had happened, and he said, "OK, I'm going to send you something called 'mood elevators.' " It's a wonderful expression, "mood elevators"—I'd never heard of "mood elevators."

He said, "You have to take them for fifteen days, and what will happen is that you will go into an even deeper depression during the first seven days, much deeper than the one in which you are now. But, whatever you do, do not stop the treatment, because if you do you've really had it. You must promise me to keep on it for a full fifteen days."

Well, I've always listened to Jean, and indeed I did go into a depression that was much, much worse for the first week. But then, after about ten days,

I was aware of a very definite, gradual improvement, and indeed, after fifteen days of treatment, I seemed to be OK. Things had changed totally for me. Jean had saved me again.

I seem to be talking only about myself and not about June. Well, that's Helmut, true to form. During this terribly depressing time, I said to June, "You may as well throw all my cameras away. I will never take another photograph." I certainly meant what I said. I was sure I would never get back to normal, I was sure I would never pick up a camera again, I was sure I would never drive a car again.

At one stage, after my course of "mood elevators," I had to go to Milan from Monte Carlo on some sort of business, not photography. I took the train from Monte Carlo in the late spring. I was sitting by the window of my compartment as we pulled out of the station, and the train wound its way along the coast for something like two hours. It was really beautiful to look at the sun setting over the Mediterranean.

The daylight lasted a long time, and a golden light fell onto the Italian coast and the little villages we traveled through. Just about thirty minutes outside Monte Carlo, we stopped at a station called Bordighera, and I fell in love with the town and the station.

It was an old turn-of-the-century watering place, a station balnéaire, which in those days must have been very fashionable. Somehow, this beautiful, tiny little place stuck in my mind. When I came back home to Monte Carlo from Milan, it started to feel a bit more like home to me. There was an inquiry from Italian *Vogue* to go and take photographs wherever I wanted. I got my cameras out and returned with my models to Bordighera.

It is now twenty years later and I am still here. Most of my work is done in and around Monte Carlo, my office looks out onto the Mediterranean Sea, and I cannot imagine living anywhere else.

I AM ENDING my story here, for to write about one's successes, small or big, is simply of no interest to the reader. Getting there is what this book is all about.

PART II: THE PHOTOGRAPHS

ABOUT MY WORK

MY PHOTOGRAPHIC EQUIPMENT

Nothing much has changed in my picture-taking technique since I was a boy. In the 1930s, I would work with daylight in the summer and in the winter I would light the portraits which I took of my girlfriends with a two-hundred-watt photo-flood bulb. Today I have graduated to a five-hundred-watt photo flood. I don't own a strobe light, rarely work in the studio—hire additional equipment and studio space whenever necessary. The "Big Nudes" are the only body of work that have been taken consistently in a studio.

My Notebooks

My memory is short, so I keep a notebook. I write ideas for future shoots, scenes from real life that catch my eye, title ideas for books and articles, very short scenarios for the next shoot which I take with me on the day. I refer to them while I work, and that way I am well prepared—though, should something better turn up while I work, I will grab it. One must not forget that models, hairdressers, stylists, makeup artists are all very expensive. And once I am out there on the street with all these people, I cannot rely on the Good Lord to send me the divine spark of inspiration. These shoots of mine are all very well prepared in advance. It is a work of many days of telephoning and meetings. The actual photography is very fast. I use one or two films and never a motor drive. Although my fees are not low, I am known to keep production costs down.

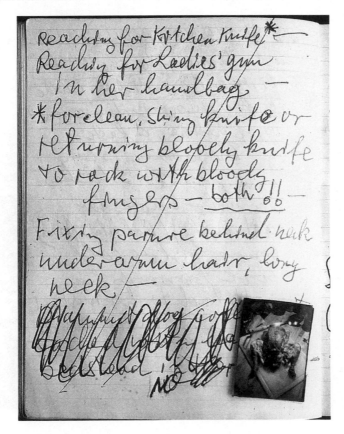

Excerpts from *World Without Men*

Recently I shot a series of photographs for the English magazine *Queen* in the attic room of my apartment. It's a tiny room, built into a tower, with small windows. I had the idea of showing a woman inside this room whilst outside, through the windows, a violent world was flying by. Fighter planes streaked through the sky, a rocket went off, there would be thunder and lightning. I arranged with Willie Landels, the art director, to montage these scenes into my pictures.

When the layouts were finished and lying on Willie's desk, Jocelyn Stevens, the owner of *Queen*, walked into the office on his return from holidaying in the Caribbean. Stevens is a colorful personality under whose direction *Queen* became a great magazine. Here is the scene as it was related to me some time later. . . .

Jocelyn sees the layouts on Willie's desk, picks them up, throws them on

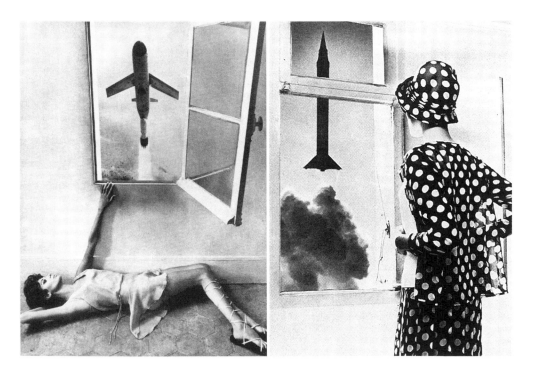

the floor, and screams: "What are these masturbating women doing in my magazine, lying on the floor, while phallic symbols are exploding outside their windows?" With this he tears the telephones out of the walls and throws them through the window.

One never knows what reaction pictures will provoke among the higher echelons at magazines. During the summer of 1971 I shot a big series of fashion photos with animals for French *Vogue*. At the time, all the prints were made and retouched in *Vogue*'s lab. One of the shots was of a model with a bear. Ten years later, I took the same negative out of the files and had it printed in my lab. When I saw the print I was very surprised. Something new had been added: the bear had a very visible erection. The powers at French *Vogue* had thought it wise to exercise some censorship and had retouched the photograph.

Strange what effect a beautiful woman has on an animal: the same happened when I photographed Lauren Hutton in 1989 with a very big alligator in Florida, and later a famous horsewoman in L.A. caressing her mount.

Store Dummies

My preoccupation with store dummies, dolls, etc., began in 1968, when English *Vogue* published my first series of photos with these dummies. It showed a favorite model of mine, Willie Van Rooy, confronting a store dummy cast in her image, thus creating a kind of Doppelgänger.

The use of these dummies allowed me to stage rather daring tableaux for French *Vogue*. Using live models would have been too risky.

MILAN, ITALY, 1968

I had promised *Uomo Vogue* to be in Milan to do some fashion photos. At the time I did not know, of course, that we were going to have a May revolution in Paris. When the time came to leave Paris, there were no trains or planes or any other means of transport leaving the city. Everything had stopped, everybody was in the street, day and night—the young people on the barricades, or marching, or making love, dressed in jeans and leather jackets, with scarves covering the lower part of their faces against the tear-gas bombs. A whole new fashion seemed to have evolved in the streets of Paris. As my Milan date approached, I wondered how I was going to get there. I had hoped that the airports would reopen, or the trains start to run again, but it didn't happen. The only way to get out was by car, but for days there was no petrol to be had, as all the pumps were closed. In my garage I had two cars: a little Austin and a big Bentley. The Bentley was almost full of petrol, and the Austin had a full tank. At the last moment June and I decided that the only way we'd make it to Milan was to take the Bentley and make for the Belgian border and then buy more petrol on the other side. It was unwise to travel during the day—the streets were still full of people demonstrating, we would never have made it. One night, around 1 a.m., I went down to the garage with a rubber tube and started sucking the petrol out of the Austin, to siphon it into the tank of the Bentley. Not being very adept at it, I got great mouthfuls of petrol and started feeling quite ill. In the end, though, the operation succeeded, and we were on our way at about three in the morning, the car almost full of petrol, the cameras and the rest of the equipment loaded into the boot. As we were nearing the border, I kept looking at the fuel gauge with anxiety—all the service stations along the route were closed; there was not a chance of getting a drop more. As we came to the customs post, the needle showed empty, but the road dipped into Belgium, and in the distance I saw the lit neon sign of a gas station. We coasted down the road and filled the car up.

Once in Milan, I decided to take my photographs in front of a big oil re-

finery. The series echoed the mood of France, the embattled factories with the young workers in front of them, like the photos I had seen in the papers back in Paris.

THE STORY OF O, 1969

I had read *The Story of O* first in the early 1960s, when I found a rare copy at one of the "bouquinistes" on the banks of the Seine. The sale of this book had been prohibited in most countries, because of its graphic descriptions of sadism and masochism. It has been a strong influence on my fashion photography, as Arthur Schnitzler and Stefan Zweig have been.

LANZAROTE, 1970

We are here on this black volcanic island to photograph a new catalogue. The hotel is typical of this resort, full of tourists, but on our first night, as we walked into the dining room, we passed a table of three people, two men and a woman, who certainly were *not* tourists. During dinner one of the men kept looking at my model. He was obviously interested in her. Later on, in the bar, the three came over to sit with us. They are a French movie director, a Hungarian scriptwriter, and his wife. They are here preparing a movie which will be filmed on the island.

As the days progress, the interest that the writer has in my model seems to increase. His wife seems not to mind, and they manage to stay near us whenever possible. As the job rather bores me, I decide to enter into the game with them. Every night, before dinner, I dress the model myself. I choose her clothes carefully, making her look more daring and risqué as the week goes on; what I don't find among the clothes we have with us to photograph, I borrow from a nearby boutique. Her skirts are getting shorter, her necklines more revealing. The writer's excitement mounts, and I become

more and more interested in my experiment in fashion; the model's attitude does not change, she stays cool but not uninterested.

It's the last evening before our departure; we all go out for dinner together. The model looks irresistible, the writer is eating her up with his eyes, the wife watches coolly and carefully. I am fascinated by the outcome of the experiment: fashion may be a superficial thing but, applied in a certain way, it can be very effective. Shortly after dinner I go to bed.

Next morning, on the airfield, we are waiting for the model. She turns up three minutes before takeoff. She looks absolutely drained. She tells me she has never had a night like this: not one second of rest.

ROME, 1970

I have always found certain pictures in the daily press inspiring. Sometimes I cut them out and keep them for a long time, and look at them over and over again. With all the intellectual questioning that has been going on in recent years about photography, many photographers hesitate so long before they take a picture that they seem never to trip the shutter. A kind of constipation has set in: maybe the day will come when the only photographers left will be the press, the others will just philosophize.

Ever since I saw *La Dolce Vita* I have been very interested in the phenomenon of the paparazzi, a totally new breed of press photographers. This is why I am now in Rome. It is only in Rome that one can find them. (*Later, of course, the idea of paparazzi photography spread all over the world.*) I have asked *Linea Italiana*, for which I am working, to arrange a contact with some of these people, as I want to hire half a dozen of them to pose with my model; and I want the real thing. So an appointment has been set up for me to meet the head man at the Caffé Greco, which is their headquarters.

At 5:00 p.m. I'm at the bar, drinking a cup of coffee with him. In front of him, next to his coffee cup, is a pack of cigarettes. He says to me: "See the man at the other end of the bar? He is a high functionary in the Intelligence

Service. He's embroiled in a big political scandal at the moment; I've been trying to get a picture of him and I just got it."

The cigarette pack contained a tiny camera, and he had been shooting the whole time we were having our coffee. I was very impressed. He explained to me that the paparazzi always work in twos. They will wait outside a restaurant where they know a certain celebrity is dining; then, when the man comes out, one of the photographers will create a scene—he might provoke him, push him a bit—the victim will get angry, protect his dinner companion, generally a glamorous woman. The paparazzo will jump out of the way, leaving the field clear for his partner to shoot the pictures fast with a flash. Very ingenious and effective.

Most of these young men with cameras are completely untrained in photography. They are country lads who come to Rome; the head man gives them cameras, explains the basic rudiments (at night working with a flash the exposure never changes, in daytime a fill-in-flash is always used—technically simple

and perfectly adequate for what certain newspapers and magazines require). What is highly developed is a network of information on who dines with whom at what place—often couples who do not wish to be seen together in public.

(Nowadays the art of paparazzi photography has become highly sophisticated. I think that the series of clandestine color photographs taken of Jackie Onassis nude, on the island of Skorpios, was probably the greatest photographic coup of the decade. It was a great technical feat and no one really knows how these pictures were obtained.)

I am introduced to the guys who will pose with my model, a price for the three-day shoot is agreed upon. I tell them that they must behave exactly as if they are stalking a celebrity, aggressive and without mercy. I tell them I will shoot very fast and get the scenes as they create them.

After the second day one of the guys comes to me and tells me that two of his colleagues have loaded their cameras with film, have taken shots of the model and me, have found out how much I am getting for my photographs, and have put together a nice little exposé, which he has sold in advance to one of the tabloids. It takes all the persuasion of an Italian friend of mine and a whopping big tip to get the rolls of film back. At the end of the third day my model is completely exhausted and hysterical from the constant pummeling, running, and goading she has undergone.

ROME, 1971

Two days before leaving Paris for Rome, I saw an advertisement in a photographic magazine that announced an interesting new little gadget: a ring flash, a contraption one screws in front of the lens which gives a soft, even light, totally shadowless. I had heard about this being used in medical photography for some time, but only for extreme close-ups as the power output was very weak. Now, this electronic flash had been improved so that one could take pictures from a distance of three to four meters, a minimum necessary for fashion work. Many years ago, Coffin, an American fashion photographer, constructed the first ring light. A big, heavy, metal-and-wooden affair, about a meter in diameter, which held about ten photo-flood bulbs. The camera was positioned immediately behind the ring, so that the lens was surrounded by the photo floods. The light quality was beautiful, the only drawback being the enormous heat which was produced by five thousand watts of electricity, and the fact that the ring was so heavy that it was hard to move around.

On my way to the airport to catch my flight, I stopped off at the camera store and bought myself one of these new marvels. That night, in Rome, I photographed evening dresses for the haute-couture report, in the boiling heat, in a long black tunnel.

Now I have the results in front of me and I am in a state of shock. The light is beautiful, the girl looks great, but to my horror she has enormous red eyes, like some kind of bat or vampire. I keep staring at the pictures. What can it be? It must be my new flash. What am I to do? Another of my snap decisions, taken at the last moment, has landed me in this horrible situation where there is no time for retakes and the pictures have to go to the printers in a rush. I

keep on staring at the film. Maybe it's not so bad, maybe it's even effective. I decide to show it to the editor. She is quite startled, looks at the pictures for a long time, and says, "OK, we'll run it, I like it." For quite some time after the Rome episode, I produced many other "red-eye" photos, until I became bored with them. I then worked out a way of avoiding them, which proved to be much more complicated than the initial discovery.

PARIS, 1972

Lately a new fashion has developed among the young fashion photographers: many of them live with their favorite model and only photograph her. They guard her jealousy and won't allow another photographer to use her. This is a situation that the magazines encourage, as it cuts down on hotel expenses when they go on location: one less hotel room to pay for.

Often the models are much better at their job than their boyfriends. It shows in the pictures. They are mechanical, and the only thing that comes across is the model's personality. This gave me an idea: I have had a machine built which is hooked up to a motor-driven camera. The machine has a timing mechanism which can be adjusted by the sitter. It's up to the model to decide whether she wants to work fast or slow. A mirror is placed next to the camera, so that she can check her pose; a strobe light is connected to my

magic box; before each exposure a bell rings and a warning light blinks: all this is designed to keep the model on her toes and to keep her excited.

I have persuaded French *Vogue* to let me do a sitting with this contraption. Carefully I explain the system to my models. I tell them, "It's up to you to control the whole sitting; you will decide when to stop, the entire responsibility is with you." Of course the lighting has been set up, and a cross where they must stand has been marked on the floor. They are totally alone in the studio, and they can only call an assistant to change the film for them. By the time the day is over, the girls are worn out; the responsibility has proved too much for them. The photos are not inspired, but quite acceptable.

I repeated the same thing for *Elle*, and it was a big success. This time I told the models to imagine that the machine was their favorite photographer and to pose in his or her style. The result was six good color pages in the magazine. The credit under the pictures reads: "La Machine de Newton."

L o s   A n g e l e s ,   1 9 7 2

I am here on an assignment for American *Vogue*, and I suddenly have some spare time. Ever since I saw Jane Russell in Howard Hughes's *The Outlaw* I have been madly in love with her. I heard that she was living nearby, so I suggested to my editor that we set up a phony sitting with her, pretend it's for the magazine, a small white lie. The editor complies and everything is set up.

We arrive at her apartment dead on time: hairdresser, makeup man, assistant, and editor. The door is opened by a lady I seem to recognize as Jane Russell. I address her as such but very quickly find out I'm wrong. She is her companion. I often have this problem, a sudden blockage in remembering a name or recognizing a face, very embarrassing, but she *does* look like her. We are informed that this is the wrong day—the appointment had been made for tomorrow. In my excitement I got the date wrong. But Miss Russell comes down the stairs and very graciously announces that, no matter, she will pose for me today.

Of course I choose her bedroom to photograph her in. We are admitted to her boudoir to begin preparations for the sitting. When it comes to choosing the dress and jewelry she will be wearing, she opens the drawers of a big commode. I am standing close to her and can see what's inside the drawers. To my delight I see that they are full of the greatest collection of wonderfully constructed, wired brassières.

There are two large Spanish beds. I ask her please to pose on one of them while I hop around the room from the other bed to a chair to the floor—to find the right angle. It's boiling hot, no air-conditioning, my T-shirt is stuck to my body, the sweat is running between my glasses and my eyes, I can hardly focus, and I'm so nervous that the camera trembles in my hands. Jane Russell poses marvelously on the bed; she looks beautiful, unchanged, cool, and collected, and she produces the most wonderful smiles. I utter the silliest cries of admiration, saying how beautiful she looks. From time to time she looks at me in a funny way. She's found out that she has a madman in her bedroom.

(I exposed three rolls of film. Every frame, except two or three, is out of focus or blurred by camera movement.)

Since then I have photographed many stars, frequently at the request of fashion editors. Many times I've wondered why, because to photograph fashion on actresses is frequently unsuccessful. Often they are too short to wear the dresses made for tall models, and temperamentally they are unsuited to sustaining long hours of posing in front of a still camera. The fashion suffers, the stars have no wish to give a lot of time to such an undertaking, and the results are mostly not worth the effort.

Some are too heavily intellectual; they will put on a dress and I will pose them in some unlikely background that pleases me, and they will ask, "What role do I play here? Who am I supposed to be?" Of course, I don't have an answer to such a question, I am not a movie director. Fashion pictures rarely have any logic; each one is a moment without a beginning or an end. There are wonderful exceptions—those stars who love clothes, love being photographed, and are untiring in front of the camera. Rampling, Deneuve, Aimée, Weaver, Loren, and Welch are such people.

Then there is the ideal sitting for an actress when it's a matter of photographing her in a certain role or doing a portrait. Not that this is easy, but it's far more satisfying and makes more sense than trying to cast an actress as a fashion model.

There is always a great fascination for me in getting a beautiful actress in front of my camera. It took days to persuade Nastassja Kinski to do a certain sitting with me, but once convinced she worked tirelessly for two days, from morning until night. Hanna Schygulla is a fascinating woman, wonderful to photograph, but she can be impatient and tricky. In 1980 I did a series of photos of her, in the role of Lili Marlene, for German *Vogue*. To present the photos to the editors I set up a projection in their Munich offices. After the showing there was dead silence. Not one of the editors uttered a word—they seemed stunned. I was perplexed: the photos were good, Schygulla looked great, technically there was no problem. I looked around the room. Then the

editor-in-chief broke the silence: "The underarm hair," she uttered. What had happened was that during the sitting Hanna had lifted her arms, and I had fallen in love with her underarm hair. I'd insisted that she keep them above her head, and the hair became an important part of my pictures. Of course, in the world of *Vogue*, there is no underarm hair, ever.

PARIS, 1974

It's late at night, and I'm taking photographs on the Place du Palais Bourbon, right outside the *Vogue* studio. Why make life hard, if one has such a great little square right on the doorstep? At night, like so many places, it takes on a special magic. I love to photograph at night. Often, when I've been on trips and have been confronted with locations that disappointed me, I

chose to photograph them by night. Everything becomes more mysterious, and all the ugliness is hidden. The very first roll of film I exposed, at the age of twelve, was shot in the Berlin Underground. I don't remember what made me do it—of course there was nothing on the film. But I learned soon enough that night photos were possible. There is always much more light than one thinks: so much so that there is great danger of overexposure. The photographs of Brassai were a great inspiration to me; he is the master of the night light, the streets of Paris, the night cityscapes, the interiors of brothels. Then there are the great pictures by Dr. Salomon, taken during soirées at embassies and at diplomatic conferences; these too have influenced me.

VILLA D'ESTE, COMO, 1975

In the spring of 1975 I went to the Villa d'Este on Lake Como. The magazine *Réalité*, a very prestigious French publication, commissioned me to make a reportage on this very famous and elegant hotel. I took two beautiful girls with me, one the daughter of a French newspaper tycoon, the other an interesting model. They both got on extremely well and played the game I wanted them to play to perfection. I decided to do two versions of this series: one for the magazine; one for my own use, to be included in my first book, *White Women*. When the book was published in 1976, it fell into the hands of the director of the Villa d'Este, Jean-Marc Droulers, and I was declared persona non grata forever. Years later he relented and invited me back and gave me and my models a wonderful banquet. Much the same happened when my second book, *Sleepless Nights*, appeared in 1978: a sequence in this book was shot in the Hotel Raphael in Paris, I also was banned from returning to that beautiful hotel, but was graciously pardoned after a very long time.

A R C A N G U E S , 1 9 7 5

I am here in this enchanting château, a few kilometers from Biarritz. The Count Guy d'Arcangues has invited me to do a series of photographs for French *Vogue* and for my first book. As always, I've been agonizing over the choice of model. For me this is the most important ingredient in my pictures.

Originally I had cast somebody else. Twenty-four hours before my departure, a girl walked into my studio in Paris. Too small for my liking, about five foot seven. She had been sent by a model agency. She's a beginner, she has no pictures to show, she has no experience, but there's something about her that fascinates me. I can't explain it. A wonderful face, a body that is really too heavy, a spark of intelligence (a rare thing but not really essential). Anyway, I know immediately that she is the one I need for my photos. A terrible risk to take—five days of concentrated work with a raw beginner. Still, I've taken this kind of risk before, and sometimes I've been sorry, but mostly my hunches have paid off.

The right girl at the right moment has always been my inspiration; it's a matter of timing. Not that I ever consider what will excite the public. If I were to do that, I would never take a picture. No, I just please myself. Long before anybody wanted to see an overweight, plump model, I begged and pleaded with the fashion editors to cut the backs of dresses so that these beauties could fit into them. It took two years for other magazines to start talking about the beauty of the big, overweight girl.

Often I'm asked to describe my perfect girl. I find that impossible to do. I know her when I see her. It's like discovering a new, unknown territory that I can explore. Also, my ideal changes drastically from time to time. In the sixties, I had a favorite model, a tall blonde German girl. I worked with her over a long period. Her body was too thin, her face angular, yet she exuded a strange sensuality, not only in her pictures but also in life. Men were completely captivated by her, followed her immediately, sensed her sexuality. There seems no rhyme or reason to all this. I have no explanation why one girl seduces my camera and another one doesn't.

HERMÈS, 1976

It was in 1976 that I decided to present to the readers of *Vogue* the Hermès boutique on the rue Faubourg St.-Honoré as the most expensive and luxuri-

ous sex shop in the world. In its glass cases there were displayed great collections of spurs, whips, leather ware, and saddles. The salesladies were
dressed like strict teachers, in wraparound gray flannel skirts, blouses closed
to the neck, and a brooch in the shape of a riding crop pinned to their bos-
oms. The president of Hermès, Robert Dumas, after seeing the *Vogue* pages,
succumbed to a malaise, but happily recovered. Later the photo of a woman
wearing a saddle illustrated an essay on "Décadence" in *Time* magazine.

ERICH VON STROHEIM, 1978

Erich von Stroheim had always been one of my heroes: inspired by his role
as the German commandant in the film *La Grande Illusion* by Renoir and
Dürrenmatt's play *La Visite de la Vieille Dame*, I started a new series of photographs of women in surgical corsets, neck braces, and casts. It was 1978.

ST.-TROPEZ, 1978

As we have done for the last fifteen years, June and I are spending the early summer in our house in Ramatuelle. This time I will be doing the ready-to-wear report for *Stern* magazine right here. I am told that all the clothes will be black, very dressy, very elegant cocktail and evening dresses. For many years I have been watching the crowds on the St.-Tropez beaches. There is no better place in the world for a voyeur like me to be constantly amused. It was here in 1969, on the Plage de la Voile Rouge, that the girls took off their bras in public for the first time. It was here that the helicopters of the Gendarmerie sprayed indelible paint on the nude sunbathers on the public beaches so they could identify them later and fine them. Every beach has its particular clientele: chic and snobby, whorish and popular, poor or family crowds. There are people from Marseille and Paris, tourists from Los Angeles

and Düsseldorf. The scene is so very familiar to me. That's why I've chosen to do the *Stern* pictures here. Often the places that I know intimately hold more mystery for me than an unknown or exotic location. I can already see the photos in my mind. Those great elegant models dressed totally in black, with hats and veils, black-stockinged legs, high-heeled black shoes, black gloves, every inch of their skin covered, amid all these half-naked men and women sunbathing on the beach.

PARIS, 1978

I'm standing on the Pont Alexandre III. It's 5 p.m., pitch black, freezing cold, driving rain. Couture-collection time. It's been like this for me now for the last twenty-four years, photographing these flimsy dresses at this impos-

sible time of the year. I know I could always go into the studio, but when I'm faced with a white-paper background, I seize up completely and don't know what to do. It's no fun. This time I've decided to do my French *Vogue* pix on store dummies. I can't possibly take real girls out in this weather. Nor can I make them stand on the railing of the bridge, not in this gale. We are all huddled up in a truck waiting for the gale to subside.

We start dressing the dummies. It's a specialist's job. I have a wizard of a girl from *Au Printemps*, who will make these mannequins take on the most wonderfully lifelike positions, with the help of cardboard and rolled-up newspaper. Part of the fun for me is to make them look as real as possible.

It's fascinating to play with these mannequins. Each one has a different personality. I often give them names. There is one that's really sexy with a submissive look in her eyes. I call her Georgette. She always comes out great in a photo. There is another one I call Le Con, which means "idiot." Whichever way I turn her, she's got a dumb look in her eyes. There is nothing I can do to make her lifelike. I decide to get rid of her. Fortunately, I have a choice of five other beauties stashed in the truck. Also about ten different pairs of legs and arms and hands.

One of them is finally dressed. We stand her up on the bridge railing, lash her down with ropes and wires so she won't fall into the Seine, should the gale blow up again. Must not see the ropes. These are color photos, and retouching in color is too expensive. Also, during the collections there is no time for these tricks. The layouts must be at the printers' in three days. It takes all night to do two photos. These mannequins are terribly hard to work with. I swear I'll never do it again.

Six months later, of course, I have forgotten all about it and I get seduced again. This time it is a new collection of mannequins that I have seen in a catalogue of Adele Rootstein's, who is a London manufacturer of store dummies (a term the lady detests). These girls are not the emaciated types favored by most dummy manufacturers, but big, buxom, six-footers with wonderful breasts and big hips. Within a short time I decide what the theme of this se-

ries of snaps with dummies will be: Nude and chained to lampposts and beautiful iron fences with the Paris cityscapes in the background. Photographed at
night in color. To top it all, June has a lovely idea. The hairdresser will have to
add pubic and underarm hair to these creatures.

PARIS, 1 9 7 9

I've had this idea in my head for some time: pictures of men and women
together, only the men are women dressed up as men. But the illusion must
be as perfect as possible, to try to confuse the reader. This man-woman am-
biguity has always fascinated me, so I submitted the idea to Kargère, the art
director of French *Vogue*, and he liked it. So here we are in the basement of
the George V; the men-women look wonderful, their waists nipped in so tight
in their elegant suits that they can hardly breathe, their short hair pomaded,
and the only truly feminine part of them that is revealed are their beautiful
hands. I have a great time taking the pictures, but the pleasure is not shared.
As the sitting progresses, through the second day, the girls become more and
more depressed; they hate the roles they're playing. At the end they say,

"Tonight we'll put on our best dresses and a ton of makeup and go dancing with the boys!"

BERLIN, 1979

I've been sent here on a great assignment: to do a series of fashion photos in my old hometown for the just-reborn German *Vogue*. There has not been a German edition since the twenties, and even then it was short-lived. This is the first attempt to relaunch it.

I'm installed at the Pension Dorian, in a side street, just off the Kurfürstendamm. I was supposed to stay either at the Kempinski or the Schlosshotel Gehrus in the Grünewald, great elegant hotels that I like a lot, but this time I felt it was more appropriate to put up in a real Berlin pension, like the one immortalized by Christopher Isherwood. The Pension Dorian is

very special—during the Nazi period it was a famous brothel, the most elegant in town, frequented by the Party bigwigs—it's very hard to get a room
here. The decor is alt Berlin—heavy, comfortable, lots of silk lampshades, big
oil paintings. I have the room off the front hall, the first door on the right as
you come in the front door. Most of the guests are theatrical folk.

During my stay I find out some interesting lore. The place is run by the
dead owner's daughter. She is about sixty-five, charming and funny, with all
that great Berlin humor that I love. One of my Berlin friends, whom I take
out to dinner on occasion, is a part-time call girl. She tells me that during the
weekends some of Kitty's old clients return to meet young women at the
pension. One room is kept exclusively for these occasions. On my way to
the bathroom I see a door open. I peer inside; the room is much bigger than
mine, the furniture more comfortable, and there is lots more silk everywhere. That's it, surely. During the weekend I keep my eyes open, and, in-

deed, I notice comings and goings of well-dressed men in their sixties, looking like they are right out of a Nazi movie.

Before leaving Paris for Berlin, I agonized for quite some time on how I should do my photos. I had asked the fashion editor if I could have only German fashions and a preponderance of lingerie. I saw little point in photographing French clothes in Berlin. Finally, June came up with a great idea: why not do all the pictures in the same places I used to frequent as a boy when I was living there? In the plane I made a list, and on arrival I took a car and checked out my locations. What is amazing is that many of the old haunts are unchanged since the twenties and thirties. Even the furniture in the beer garden, where I photographed the lederhosen scene, seemed exactly the same.

The underwear shop in the Nürnbergerstrasse appeared unreal today. The scenes around the lakes, with girls in their underwear, reminded me of early days when we went swimming in the lake and we took our clothes off by the bank. It seemed as if I had stepped into the past. I was lucky with the light—big black clouds hung over the city every day—it was very intense and sharp, what I call "black light."

"Big Nudes," 1980

In 1980 I made a number of photographic series on these themes:

The "Big Nudes" began in 1980 and were inspired by police identity photos of German terrorists. I intermittently made twenty-one of these images until 1993. Also in 1980 I began the "Naked & Dressed," which I abandoned by 1990 because as a photographic exercise it was technically too difficult to continue.

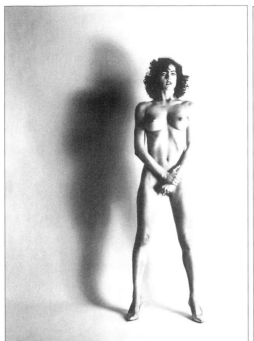

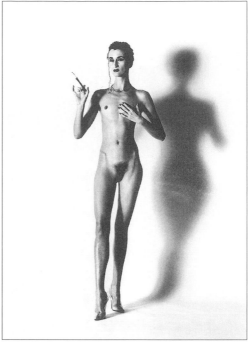

SAUMUR, 1980

In the caserne of the Cadre Noir. French *Vogue* have asked me to do a series of photographs of Versace clothes for the September issue. I asked the fashion editor on the sitting to describe the styles to me. They sounded vaguely military—jodhpurs, riding breeches, leather. I had an idea that this could work with a crack cavalry regiment. I wondered, does such a unit still exist in the French army? I asked the editor. (Her connections in the upper strata of French society are very good.) She informed me that indeed there exists within the French army an elite corps of horsemen. Permission might be very difficult to obtain. A few days later, I received a call from the office: I had the green light.

We drive out to Saumur for the day to have a look around. It's a very beautiful place; great buildings and a wonderful old riding school. I see officers exercising their horses. It looks OK, but will it make a picture? I don't care much for horses, but the men look beautiful in their black uniforms—with no pockets, so that the lines of their bodies are unbroken. I have rarely seen such elegance: the way they walk, stand, strike poses, not to speak of how they look on their horses. The strange thing, though, they all seem to be chain smokers; some use elegant black cigarette-holders. Even while they're riding they're smoking. But where the hell do they keep all these cigarettes if they have no pockets?

A week later, we go out to take the photographs. The sitting is scheduled to last for two days, which is my ideal working time. My attention seems to flag after the second day and I get bored. I put this down to my superficial nature. This is why I could never do movies: to give a month, maybe a year to one project seems impossible to me. The beauty of photography is that it's comparatively cheap to produce, can be done quickly with the minimum of personnel and equipment, and if you screw up one job there is always another one that might work out. Also, one does not have to get up early in the morning.

I have decided to play down the horse element, and to concentrate, rather, on those elegant men, but I need a lot of these guys to make the picture work.

This presents quite a problem. Then I have to convince the colonel that I need his men for two days. Then I have to explain to them that a fashion photograph is not done in two minutes, but takes some time. I don't tell them how much time—it might frighten them off. I have done all this before, and it's the hardest part of the job. I work in a peculiar manner. I shuffle people around like other photographers do with still life. It takes time.

I start work. I've got about five men, not nearly enough. As we go along, I see others come across the parade ground. I get the editor to round up any officer who seems aimless or not usefully employed. By lunchtime I am doing well—I've got about fifteen men. That's really good. Now to keep their attention, get them enthusiastic, make them pose without giggling and laughing, to try and build up a photograph around my two models. By 3 p.m. I've got two pictures done. It's a strain and tricky, but the guys look wonderful and pose beautifully. In fact, they look a lot more interesting than the models. Sleeker, more authority, absolutely believable.

It's my models that are the problem. Or is it the clothes? But never mind,

I have to press on, must do four pages a day. I decide to do the whole article in spreads; that means I'll only have to do four photos for my eight pages. That always sounds so good, so easy. I should know better. I'm going mad trying to push these people around to fit them into the frame of my camera. I'm also looking for signs of flagging attention and terrible boredom. If I lose them now, I've had it. But all is well, no casualities, and around 6 p.m., as the light fades, I've done my quota.

The next morning there are quite a few deserters. The men have decided that it's a lot more fun to be a cavalry officer on duty than a model. I have six men left, that's all. Now the only way is to ask them to get their horses and mount them. Those horses will fill up the frame, make today's photos look different from yesterday's, and maybe add a new excitement. But by the time everything is in its place—the riders look great and the girls look beautiful— the horses' ears droop, and their long-lashed eyes are half closed, like they're asleep. But the light is beautiful, the sun is strong and hard, and there are beautiful clouds in the sky. One can't have everything.

By 5 p.m. it's done and we pack up. During the lunch hour an officer takes me aside. He's taken a shine to one of my girls, a five-foot-ten blonde with a beautiful mouth. I had her hair done in a thick blond braid wound around her head (a hairstyle I like and use from time to time); she looks magnificent. The officer has a request. He wants me to take her photograph sitting naked on a horse inside one of the riding schools. He assures me we will be alone and undisturbed.

I ask the girl. She's amused by this and says she'll do it. I just love this guy and his daydreams. We set an hour for this extracurricular work. But just when we're about to start, the general arrives to visit us all. The officer discreetly tells me it's no go. What a pity. This could have been a great picture.

CHIRAC, 1981

In 1981 I was hired by the advertising agency that was managing Jacques Chirac's first presidential campaign to take his portrait for an election poster. At the time he was mayor of Paris. He was charming to me. I asked him

please to change his blue shirt for a white one, which I thought would be more chic, but he demurred. I kept on insisting, and in the end he gave in. A reading lamp was on his desk, which also I did not like. So I got hold of it, trying to move it; I yanked at it a number of times with all my might while Chirac looked at me with unbelieving eyes, until I realized the lamp was screwed onto the desk. It turned out that Madame Chirac was quoted as saying, "I don't recognize my Jacques on this photo," and according to the agency another photographer's portrait was chosen, not as good as mine.

Working from the Wheelchair, 1981

In 1981 I made all my models march and run at great speed through the Paris streets. I remember well that one day at the Trocadéro, a favorite location of mine, when we were all racing downhill I was thrown out of my wheelchair twice. This did not stop me from carrying on—after all, I had paid for this wheelchair for six months.

PARIS, 1981

My immediate surroundings are always more mysterious and exciting to
me than some faraway place. Now that I am living near the Luxembourg
Gardens, I spend a lot of time taking photos there, walking around doing
nothing—just looking, watching the people—every little corner is familiar
and beautiful.

One day June and I were wandering around aimlessly; I had an urge to
pee. I made for my favorite pissotière, just a few meters off the main walk.
One can see the heads of the men sticking up over the little wall against
which one pees; a gentle stream of water constantly runs down the wall. As
I pee I look over the wall and see June watching me, waiting for me to finish.
People stroll by, it's idyllic, where else but in France could this happen? I said
to June: "I simply must do a fashion picture here. How wonderful to have an

elegantly dressed woman waiting for her escort, watching him the way you watched me just now."

A few months later, during one of our walks, we passed by the big hot-house where they keep the palm trees when it gets cold. People sit and sun-bathe there; it's the most sheltered spot in the Luxembourg. On this day one of them is a woman about fifty, an umbrella shading her face; she wears a black tailored suit with tight skirt, no stockings, but high black leather boots, her legs apart. As we pass, I take her in from head to toe and I don't believe my eyes: she is stark naked under her skirt, and I think I can see her pussy. About fifty meters farther on, I recover and tell June what I thought I saw.

"You're making it up," she says, "it's your lurid imagination."

"OK," I say, "let's go back and check." We turn around and go back, and, indeed, there it is, as large as life. June wants me to go and get my camera, but I can't do that. I am no reporter. I file this image in my head: one day I'll reproduce it.

H O L L Y W O O D ,   1 9 8 5

For a long time during my annual sojourn in Hollywood I photographed a lot of actresses, some talented others not, for *Vanity Fair*. They were invari-ably accompanied by their press agents, who became more and more de-

manding and obnoxious, standing behind me, looking over my shoulder while I was photographing their charges, saying, "Not from this angle, make her head turn to the right, you are showing too much skin, cover your shoulders," and demanding photo approval, which I have only ever granted on two occasions: Elizabeth Taylor and Madonna, both intelligent women. After I banned all press agents from my sittings, there were no more of these shoots; instead I was photographing actors and producers, marvelously interesting faces that fascinated me. Also, I asked *Vanity Fair*'s then editor-in-chief, Tina Brown, to let me photograph criminals, murderers, and politicians.

PORNO, 1985

In 1985, during our usual wintering period in Hollywood, I met a very attractive young couple at a cocktail party at Timothy and Babs Leary's house. I got talking to them, and they knew about some of my so-called sexy photographs. They offered to pose for me while they were fucking. Like many photographers, I had toyed with the idea of making pornography. But I always hesitated, having an inbuilt safety brake that, after all these years with *Vogue,* stopped me from crossing that threshold. But then I decided I needed to overcome my resistance and to have a shot at it. This couple and another Los Angeles couple, equally good-looking, were my only attempts into this field. In both cases the people concerned signed a release which gave me the right to publish these photos. Many years later, my dealer brought a collector of pornography to my office in the hope that he would buy some of these photos. After looking carefully through the lot, he looked at me and said, "Mr. Newton, these photos are not hard enough for my collection." Though one pleased him a little bit, he hated the lamp on the left of the picture, and asked me if I could retouch it out. When I asked him what he had against the lamp, he said he was a furniture dealer and the lamp offended him.

DALÍ, 1986

In 1986, *Vanity Fair* sent me to Figueras to photograph Dalí in his own museum. He knew I preferred photographing with daylight, so he let me cool my heels in my hotel for two days and called me into his presence on the third day, when the weather forecast was for severe storms. He was beautifully coiffed, dressed in a silver satin robe, and wearing the highest order bestowed on him by the King of Spain.

When the sky turned black, Dalí said, "I'm ready for Newton, who is here because he knows I'm dying." There was no more daylight, I had to get my one five-hundred-watt photo-flood bulb out to take this historical last photo of him for *Vanity Fair*.

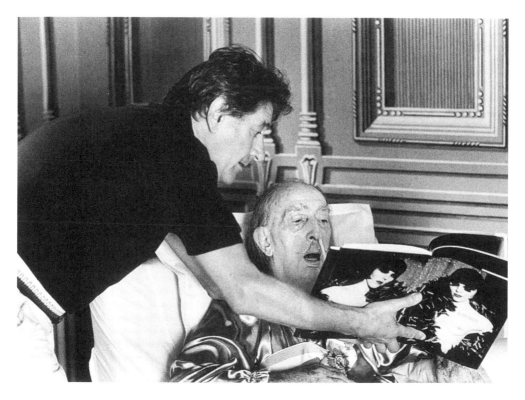

My Magazine, 1987

In 1987 I departed on the ultimate ego trip: I decided to publish a magazine, which would contain thirty-two photographs and would be called *Helmut Newton's Illustrated*. My art director was June. I am quoting from the introduction to the first issue: "In my mind I've been recalling early Berlin pictorial journalism of the '20s and '30s, publications like the *Berliner Illustrirte Zeitung* and others, which were part of my daily life as a young man."

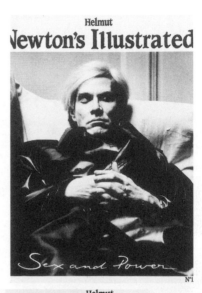

WALDHEIM, 1988

In 1988, Tina Brown sent me to Vienna to photograph Austria's President Kurt Waldheim. He had become a controversial figure because of his Nazi past. With me, to conduct the interview, was the great writer Gregor von Rezzori. Next morning we arrived at the Presidential Schloss, and while we waited for the President, the aide-de-camp showed me the places where I was allowed to photograph him. The choice was very small; the light was terrible, of course; I had no additional lighting except a reflector, relying on the tiny bit of daylight that seeped through the windows on that gray day. So, when Waldheim arrived, I squeezed him between a window and a wall and started to shoot away. All the time, he had a sinister grin on his face, so I asked him to be serious. He said he did not like serious photos of himself. So I thought to myself, "If he wants to look sinister, that's OK by me, let him hang himself." Anyway, once the shoot was over, he was so sweet to me and invited me to his box at the opera that evening. I warned him that I only had one pair of jeans with me, no tie, and an old jacket. He said, "Don't worry." So I arrived at the opera after the curtain had gone up, was ushered into his box, saw that there was a black

man on the stage, and divined that this was *Otello*. Waldheim was there with two ladies, one somewhat older than the other. So I sat next to the older one, thinking that was the missus. She realized my mistake and said, "I am not the one," so I sidled up to the younger one and apologized for my faux pas, saying, "I did not think that the Frau President was so young and good-looking." Now, Tina had told me to try and get a photo of the Waldheims together, and here was the golden opportunity to ask her. She was charming and said, "Yes, come to our house for breakfast tomorrow morning and we will pose for you."

HELMUT KOHL, 1990

In September 1990 I went to Bonn to make a portrait of German Chancellor Helmut Kohl. It was a cold and rainy day. I had a good look at Kohl's offices, which did not inspire me in any way. In desperation I looked out of the

window at the park below; miraculously, the rain had stopped, so I took a walk around the park trying to find a big German oak. All the oaks were thin and looked like toothpicks, but the elms were big. I chose the biggest, and posed the Kanzler before it. He was a willing and charming model and gave me all the time I needed. When I said, "Thank you, that's it, Herr Bundeskanzler," he replied, "Mr. Newton, now, please, take a picture of me with *my* Rhine."

MRS. THATCHER, 1991

Margaret Thatcher had always fascinated me. There was a woman who was strong and powerful, and as she became more successful and more powerful, she seemed to me to become even sexy. Shortly after she abdicated, she came to Anaheim, California, to give a lecture before hundreds of people. It was the year 1991, and Tina arranged for her to sit for me. I drove there very early in the morning, arriving at the hotel where Thatcher and her entourage were staying, around 8:30 a.m. The hotel gave me a large suite which would serve as my studio, but my idea was to photograph her by the pool. For a long time I had a kind of crush on her; all that power had a strong effect on me, and I wanted to show my admiration by presenting her with the most gorgeous roses I could buy. I raced to the hotel's flower shop. It was closed—too early. I returned three times; at last the door was open, and inside were lots of tired roses. I bought every one in the shop, raced upstairs, and waited for my prey. Every time I heard somebody coming down the corridor toward my suite, I raced to the door, carrying armfuls of tired roses, ready to open the door and confront my goddess. At last she arrived, wearing a nice suit, with her legs nylon-clad, her hair coiffed in a bouffant style, and not one hair out of place. I was sweating with excitement and nervousness; she was cool and collected. I presented my roses, which she graciously accepted and handed to her aide-de-camp, a very nice young man. I suggested we should go to the pool; she declined, in a rather stern voice. There was a gale blowing, and she was not going to get that hair out of place. I asked her would she please sit on this

chair and cross her legs. Her legs were not bad at all. She sat down but did
not cross her legs. I put my little old Fuji camera on my tripod; she cocked
her head and smiled kind of sourly at my lens. I asked her to straighten her
head and please be serious. She replied, "Oh, but one looks so disagreeable
when one does not smile." At last she stopped smiling, and I clicked the shutter. Everything was over. She left royally. Five minutes later her aide-de-camp
returned, and I asked him to sign the release which gives the magazine the
right to publish a person's picture. He said, "Mr. Newton, we never sign; you

may print any of the photos you have taken of the Prime Minister." Mrs.
Thatcher was so much in command of the event, she would never make one
wrong move or give anything away. As it turned out, she hated the photo and
reminded me of that at every meeting that we later had. I loved the picture—
she looked like a shark, her head was straight on her shoulders, and she was
unsmiling. The photograph is now hanging in the National Portrait Gallery in
London, a large print, two meters high.

"D O M E S T I C   N U D E S ,"   1 9 9 2

I love my winters in the Château Marmont in Hollywood, where June and
I have stayed for the last twenty-six years. I have this fascination for familiar
surroundings. My favorite photos are often those which evoke a strong feel-

ing of "I have been here before." The "Domestic Nudes" series began by my wanting to photograph the rooms of the Château Marmont that I know so well, but who would look at my pictures of empty rooms? So I added naked women.

LE PEN, 1997

Neuilly sur Seine, April 1997. I am here in Jean-Marie Le Pen's house to photograph him for *The New Yorker*. His reputation as an extreme rightist and anti-Semite has been well established. Just the kind of guy I love to photograph. And I do mean this. I am sitting in his salon, waiting to be called into his presence. On the wall a naval painting, on a table a large Holy Bible, elaborately printed and illuminated. Should be good for a shot. Like always, I have to make the guy love me if I want to get a good portrait. Making people's portraits is an act of seduction on the photographer's part. That's what I always tell myself in this kind of situation. And, indeed, Le Pen and I get on like a house on fire: he loves me, I love him. The sitting starts in the garden. He is patient and pliable until I see two big Dobermans. Something goes click in my head; I ask him to pose with the dogs. He says "No," his daughter who is present, says "No way," but after a short back and forth, there he is, posing lovingly like a lamb, with those dogs.

THE QUEEN, 2000

May 4, 2000, was the opening of the new wing of the National Portrait Gallery in London. I and many other photographers and artists were invited to attend. We were to stand next to our works with our subjects. So there I was, standing to attention by my portrait of Lady Thatcher, and she on the other side, as far away from me as possible. She had told me previously how much she disliked this image and took this opportunity to repeat her critique in detail. Now, I own only one suit, which I wore on that day. As I walked through the portals of the National Portrait Gallery, I heard a "plop" and an enormous glob of pigeon shit landed on my right shoulder. The stink was horrible. I had two pieces of Kleenex, already used, in my pocket, with which I tried to wipe off the shit. It only made it worse. You can see the marks clearly on the photo.

LENI RIEFENSTAHL, 2000

Vanity Fair sent me to do yet another portrait of Leni Riefenstahl. We met first in Havana in 1987 and started a rather strange relationship: I admired her greatly as a filmmaker and photographer, and she seemed flattered that a German Jewish, somewhat notorious photographer was really interested in her. As a schoolboy, I saw all her movies, like *The Blue Light*, *The White Hell of Piz Palü*, etc. These were mostly films about the German mountains, heroic skiers and pilots, snow and glaciers.

The Berliners referred to her at that time as the "Reichsgletscherspalte"—hard to translate, but it means roughly "German Reich's glacier cunt or vagina"—because they were sure that Hitler and she were lovers, which, of course, was not true, but Leni surely was pretty crazy about Hitler.

I knew her work intimately and often mentioned her in my lectures. I got a lot of flak from people, June included, who can't understand how a Jew could have that kind of relationship with a person who has such a dubious political past. I seem to be able to separate the person from the work.

At a recent lecture I referred to her as an important artist, though an old Nazi. When I arrived at her house, near Munich, in June 2000 for the last sitting, she sat me down at a big table laden with coffee and cake, took my hand, held it in hers without letting go—and this lady of ninety-nine had an iron grip—and, waving a newspaper report in my face, said, "Helmut, promise me never to call me an old Nazi again or else I will not let you photograph me ever again." Well, what could I do? Being an old *pute* (whore) and thinking only of the pictures I was hoping to get that day, I would have promised to marry her. So we started our sitting. Leni was wearing pants, and I know she is very proud of her legs and thinks they are better than Marlene Dietrich's, so I asked her to change into a skirt. Well, the pants came off in a jiffy and she was in the shortest skirt. As they say, "The legs are the last to go."

SCHRÖDER'S DINNER, 2000

My eightieth birthday turned out to be a great event for me: the German Center for Photography, under the direction of Manfred Heiting, invited me to do a major retrospective show in Berlin, and they offered me the Neue Nationalgalerie, a great building by Mies van der Rohe, what an honor. I asked June to curate the show, and she did a brilliant job and everybody said so. It was surely the most beautiful exhibition I ever had or am likely to have. And in a place that is also famous for being a beautiful but extremely difficult space.

We spent ten days in Berlin before the show opened to supervise the last prints, using a process called "High Density Laser Prints," which proved to be the most ball-breaking experience. We were in the plant for days and nights, at times until 3 a.m., tearing up print after print. We often went to the Paris Bar for dinner. One night I almost failed to recognize Gerhard Schröder, the Chancellor of Germany, as he and his family left the bar, but while he was being photographed by the paparazzi outside on the street, he recognized me through the window and came back in to say hello and invite June and me for

dinner. He called me "Mr. Newton," and I said, "Please, Herr Bundeskanzler, call me Helmut," to which he said, "Only if you call me Gerd." Then we all trooped out to take snaps.

Well, the official invitation arrived by fax the next day at the hotel. I proudly propped it up on the desk in our room, read it, and said to June, "Let's stay an extra day in Berlin and go and dine at Gerd's house Thursday." So, Thursday night, we get our driver to take us to the residence, dozens of white roses in the trunk of our car, present of an admirer, which we intended to present to Madame.

When we arrived at the house, a smart German officer asked what we had come for and I said "dinner," to which he replied, "Herr Newton, that was last night, with the Herr Kulturminister Naumann." I thought I was going to have a heart attack. June was very elegant about it, tried to calm me down. If she had made this blunder I probably would have killed her.

All the way back, I was ranting that the date on the invitation was for Thursday and "they" had made the mistake and "they" can't get their act together and that's why they lost the war, thank God, and the last one they won was in 1871. I raced up to the room, checked the date on the fax—it was for Wednesday.

The next day, I rang the Chancellor to apologize, and Gerd said, "Too bad, you missed a really good dinner, and we waited for you for ages." I never heard from Gerd again.

My Relationship with Printers, 2001

The printing of a black-and-white image is a dying art. I know *very* few guys in France and America that are capable of satisfying my particular style. These people have to be nurtured, praised, and coddled. They are fragile and often strange, and my relationship with them has to be sometimes that of a lover. My theory is that, if a guy spends his life in a room lit only by a dim orange lamp or in total blackness, his behavior must be a bit bizarre.

I remember a very fine printer, Marc Picot at Central Color in Paris, whom, unwittingly, I must have hurt; consequently, he informed me that our relationship was ended and he would never print my negatives again. Anyway, I had to take Marc to a special lunch, practically go down on my knees, and beg forgiveness. He forgave me and continued his great work for me.

During the year 2001, I was preparing an exhibition entitled "Sex & Landscapes." Every image was 160 X 120 cm large, and many negatives were complicated to print. There were fifty-five works, each in an edition of three plus one Artist Proof.

Choi, a master printer with whom I had worked for years and had an ex-

cellent relationship, had the task of producing these prints over many months. I had to make a great number of trips to Paris to check the work, and was very tired during the last session in the lab, and must have spoken with a wrong tone of voice to him when I refused to accept certain prints. I returned to Monte Carlo and was informed the next day by his partner that Choi had run out of the lab in tears, only to return there two days later, still upset; it was decided that they would never accept my work again.

I had to deliver all these prints at a certain date, and I was desperate. What could I do but once more eat humble pie, write a letter of apology, and on the next trip embrace and kiss Choi twice on each cheek.

ART AND COMMERCE

I have some good friends who are "fine-art" photographers. They refuse any kind of commission and only work for themselves, in the hope of a grant or a sale to a museum. I admire their steadfastness but often find their pictures boring. I have to thank the commercial world—the "consumer society"—for whatever success I have had, not foundations, museums, or grants. I have always found stimulus and inspiration in working for magazines or commissions. I seem to need this kind of discipline and a definite framework in which to work. Of course, I often suggest certain ideas to editors in the hope that they will let me realize them. I find the editorial page acts for me as a kind of "think tank" or laboratory to try out new ideas. How else could I draw on the services of the best makeup artists, hairdressers, and models that the world has to offer? I couldn't function without their help. Had it not been for the adventurous spirit of French *Vogue* in publishing my work when it was still considered daring, the evolution of my photography would have been much slower.

When I take pictures I don't do it just for myself, to put them away in a drawer. I want as many people as possible to see them. There is an excitement in the diversity of going from editorial work, to commercial assignments, to the production of books and exhibitions. Because I've put down the concept of "fine-art" photography, during lectures and workshops I have been asked, "Why, then, do you give exhibitions in art galleries?" Though it is wonderful to exhibit in a beautiful, prestigious gallery, it would be equally exciting to show in some big white garage, or any other space that would lend itself as a background for photographs. Exhibitions are such a change from the printed page: one deals with an entirely different dimension. Original prints, either small or large, make an entirely different impact on the public. Just as a magazine is ephemeral, so a book is like a house: it's there for a long time. Each is a different discipline.

POLAROID PHOTOS

When I get my Polaroid camera ready, I always have a strange feeling:
Before the invention of this incredible gadget, the masters did their work
without it, and they produced unforgettable pictures. Why do I need this
crutch? And how come the first Polaroids often contain a freshness and spon-
taneity that is lacking in the carefully planned final shots on what I call "real
film"? Here's the reason: I get impatient to see what my picture will look like,
I grab the camera, hold it any old way, straight or at an angle, and just squeeze
the shutter.

I never use Polaroids on portrait sittings. The person always wants to see
what he or she looks like, and if what people see doesn't please them they become unhappy and insecure, and I have to start wooing and seducing them all
over again in order to restore their confidence in themselves and me.

It's a wonderful sketch pad, the Polaroid. I use it often to take my "first
look" at what I am about to do. Do I like what I see? Do I want to continue
in this way, or do I change my tactics? Somewhere along the line, and rather
sooner than later, I must make a decision on how I want the sitting to go—
in what direction. The Polaroid helps me—though I've been known to make
the wrong choices and not continue and later regret it.

At times I use the Polaroid like the early explorers used beads to win the
confidence of the natives: I give them to people to ensure their cooperation.
I hand them out as souvenirs—anything to get my way. But generally I spend
as little time on them and do as few as possible. Maybe one or two. It's more
important to me to spend the time in getting something on real film. There
was one exception! When I worked on "The Naked and the Dressed," maybe
the most complicated series of photos I have ever produced, I used boxes of
the stuff. My assistant stood next to my camera and shot as many Polaroids as
he could at the same time as I photographed, so that I could be sure to get the
same movement for the second version. One must realize the difficulty in

matching the same movement of legs, feet, hands, heads, and expressions when a group or even *only* a single person moves rapidly in front of the camera—and also the fact that the time lag between the versions is often as long as two or three hours.

Hair and makeup have to be rechecked—people have to eat, and by then much of the initial drive has flagged. Also, if I didn't have many Polaroids to refer to, it would be impossible to match up the two versions.

"Reconstruction is the next best thing to being there." I was in the apartment of a woman in Los Angeles having a drink with her. At one moment, she picked up a cigarette lighter in the shape of a revolver, and after lighting her cigarette, she stuck the thing in her mouth and looked at me. I took a quick shot. A year later I put this on real film.

Of course, at times, like all photographers, I use the Polaroid to check some technical details, complicated lighting setups, stuff like that; and in these cases it is also a tremendous help.

RETURN TO BERLIN

Well, it looks like a fait accompli that my archives will go to my home-town. The Lord Mayor of Berlin, Klaus Wowereit, has taken me to his heart and has given me an absolute palace in which to establish the Helmut Newton Foundation. It is he and Professor Klaus-Dieter Lehmann, president of the Prussian Heritage Foundation, who have cut through all the official red tape to make this happen.

The story of how this came about is not without drama. On a trip to Berlin in 2002, we were shown five buildings—each one more depressing than the other—that the authorities said could be available for my archives, until at the end of the long day when our guides had almost given up, they announced that there was one more building to see, but assured us that we wouldn't like it. Tired and exhausted, we piled into the car and headed for the heart of West Berlin, near the Hardenbergstrasse where I used to go for those gymnastic lessons, five minutes away from the Kempinski, a part of Berlin that I know like the back of my hand. We stopped at the back entrance to the beautiful Zoological Gardens and the Zoo Train Station. And what do I see before me? A palace! A beautiful three-story, early-twentieth-century building, its façade magnificent. Engraved on the top of this palace is the legend: "Built during the reign of the German Kaiser Wilhelm II, King of Prussia, for the Officers of the Army in Berlin 1909."

We were led into the building, and more wonders: it is in almost perfect condition, like it was waiting for me. From the windows I can see across the road to the railroad station to the quay, from where I said goodbye to my parents sixty-four years ago to go out into the wide, wide world. I am not a sentimental guy, but I could not suppress a certain frisson as that day came back to me.

LIST OF ILLUSTRATIONS

A NOTE ABOUT THE AUTHOR

HELMUT NEWTON, born in Berlin in 1920, developed a distinctive aesthetic in his photographs of fashion models and nudes. He is one of the most stubborn, idiosyncratic and admired photographers of the twentieth century. He has received numerous awards, including the Grand Prix National de la Ville de Paris (1990), the Grosses Bundesverdienstkreuz of the Federal Republic of Germany (1992), Commandeur de l'Ordre des Arts et des Lettres (1966), and Officier de l'Ordre de Mérite Cultural de Monaco (2001). Today Helmut Newton and his wife, June, live in Monte Carlo.

A NOTE ABOUT THE TYPE

The text of this book is set in Perpetua, a typeface designed by Eric Gill and released by the Monotype Corporation between 1925 and 1932. This typeface has a clean look with beautiful classical capitals, making it an excellent choice for both text and display settings. Perpetua was named for the book in which it made its first appearance: *The Passion of Perpetua and Felicity.*